The State and Organised Labour in Botswana

'Liberal Democracy' in emergent capitalism

MONAGENG MOGALAKWE

Ashgate

Aldershot • Brookfield USA • Singapore • Sydney

Published by
Ashgate Publishing Ltd
Gower House
Croft Road
Aldershot
Hants GU11 3HR
England

HD
6873
.M64
1997

Ashgate Publishing Company
Old Post Road
Brookfield
Vermont 05036
USA

British Library Cataloguing in Publication Data

Mogalakwe, Monageng
The state and organised labour in Botswana : 'liberal democracy' in emergent capitalism. - (The making of modern Africa)
1. Labor supply - Botswana 2. Trade-unions - Botswana
3. Botswana - Economic conditions - 1966 -
I. Title
331.1'1'096883'09046

Library of Congress Catalog Card Number: 97-70888

ISBN 1 85972 344 6
Printed in Great Britain by the Ipswich Book Company, Suffolk

Contents

Tables and figures   vi
Acknowledgements   vii

Introduction   1
1 Theorising the state-labour relation   6
2 Botswana: an overview and rapid assessment   25
3 The Botswana state in historical perspective   33
4 The capitalist form of the Botswana state   54
5 The state and the trade unions   68
6 Labour law and industrial relations   80
7 Trade union growth and development   98
8 Class organisation and class struggles   115
9 Prospects for organised labour in the 1990s and beyond   131

Bibliography   143
Index   151

Tables and figures

Table 3.1   Selected social and economic indicators   41

Table 3.2   Gross domestic product by type of economic activity
             (percentage of total)   44

Table 3.3   Ownership of manufacturing firms (selected years)   49

Table 4.1   Estimated earnings by economic activity and citizenship
             of employees (March 1991)   61

Table 7.1   Estimated number of paid employees by sector and
             economic activity, 1986-95 (selected years)   100

Table 7.2   Registered trade unions and estimated membership
             (January 1996)   102

Figure 4.1 Lorenz curves for 1985-86 and 1993-94   64

Acknowledgements

During the course of writing up this book I have incurred debts of gratitude to many people who gave me encouragement, advice, and assistance and criticized this work at various stages of its preparation. These people are too numerous to mention them by name, but my special thanks go to Robert Fine, Peter Gutkind, Robin Cohen, Keith Jeffries, Bojosi Otlhogile, Taufila Nyamadzabo, Lawrence Tshuma and Tetteh Hormeku-Ajei. My special thanks also go to Krassi Petrova who expertly prepared and typeset the book. Frank Youngman painstakingly looked at chapter drafts and made always well informed and constructive comments. However, I take the sole responsibility for shortcomings. I would also like to thank my employer, the University of Botswana, for the financial support. Last but not least, my thanks go to my daughters Bothepha and Segopodiso and their mother Koketso who endured with fortitude many hours of my absence.

Introduction

The thesis of this book is that even in a formally liberal democratic country, the imperatives of economic growth and development in a capitalist context give rise to the state's close supervision and control of organised labour. This constitutes a repressive structure of social relations that is maintained by the state through the exercise of political power and legitimated through an ideology of national interest. The corollary of this argument is that these structures of repression only set limitations to working class actions; they do not prevent them. My starting point is that the motive force of history is constituted primarily by changes in the modes of production, the consequent division of society into distinct classes, and the struggles of these classes against one another.

The repressive structures of social relations are, however, historically specific and contingent upon the balance of various social forces. Marx (1968a) pointed out that people make their own history, although they do not make it as they please but under circumstances directly encountered, given and transmitted by the past. Following Marx, it can be argued that even within those structural limits, some amount of economic and political struggle is possible. That is to say, there exists an area of choice in the structure of social relationships, even if this choice can occur only within definite limits. Moreover, these limits tend to relax as the level of technical and economic development rises and the working class increases its social weight (Hyman, 1975; Fine, 1991).

The repressive structures of social relations constitute forms of labour control by the state on behalf of capital, whilst industrial action in its various forms constitutes resistance to the capitalist control of the labour process. As Crisp (1984) argues, following Marx, labour control and labour resistance are integral and inseparable features of the capitalist mode of production; they presuppose the existence of each other, condition the existence of each other, and reciprocally bring forth each other. Central to my analysis is the dialectical relationship between structure and agency, and a recognition that social structures are transformable through the actions of actors caught up in those structures.

1

The state-labour relation is interactive: the state influences the labour movement by imposing political limits upon it, but the labour movement in turn influences the state by its struggles from below. In a class divided society in which the means of production are largely in the hands of certain individuals, there is bound to be a clash of interests between the class that owns the means of production and those who only own their labour power. In this type of society, the state comes to rely on the taxes and revenues from the economically dominant classes to the extent that the state becomes indebted to this class or alliance of classes. Because of this relationship, the state tries to sustain this type of social order by declaring universal legitimacy of the narrow interests of this class, and by representing its interests as the common interests of all members of society (Marx and Engels, 1970, p. 65).

The form in which particular class interests are presented as the general interests of society is through the ideology of nationalism. The prevalent ideological forms are those of "national interest" and "national development". Ideology is used in this context to refer to a particular form of human thinking that conceals class contradictions of society in metaphysical abstractions, and tends to present the society as a harmonious entity (Billig, 1982, p. 32).

This book is a departure from the conventional analyses on Botswana's political economy, which have been limited to the descriptive analyses of economic growth and structural transformation. For my part, I delve beneath these descriptions and dominant conceptual frames to reveal the character of a system of labour repression. I view the process of economic development and the relations of production which characterise this process as constituting a terrain of class struggle in which the interests of capital accumulation are in conflict with the interests of the working class. I also move beyond the current analyses of the political economy of Botswana by showing how the economic growth and structural changes that have occurred in Botswana in the last 30 or so years were accompanied by processes of class formation and class conflict.

The process of economic growth and structural changes also shapes classes, which becomes as much an outcome as a starting point of the process of accumulation (Richards and Waterbury, 1990, p. 10). I examine the class character of the Botswana state and argue that the postcolonial economic policies must be seen as a class project of the nascent national bourgeoisie which now has structural links with the political elite. I give the previously static description of economic growth and structural transformation a new dynamics by situating this process within the context of the capitalist mode of production and its attendant social relations. This is one aspect that the current literature on Botswana has not addressed.

Botswana's peripheral capitalist development can be divided into three distinct phases. The first phase was that of Botswana's integration into the world capitalist system through colonialism. This lasted up to the time of formal political independence. The second phase of Botswana's capitalist development was from Independence in 1966 to 1990. This is the focal point of my analysis. This period was characterised by direct state intervention in the economy and in industrial relations. At the economic level, the state intervened through creating a physical

2

and social infrastructure and establishing public enterprises in various sectors of the economy. At the level of industrial relations, the state intervened through a restrictive wages policy and labour legislation. The first wages policy was in place for close to twenty years from 1972 to 1990. The third phase of Botswana's capitalist development emerged in the 1990s after the adoption of the 1990 *Report of the Presidential Commission on the Review of the Incomes Policy* (hereinafter, Presidential Commission). The third phase of Botswana's capitalist development is characterised by changes which appear to indicate a transition from state interventionism to a more neoliberal form of state involvement in the economy.

I begin in Chapter 1 by critically exploring some of the Marxist debates on the state. In this section I develop a theoretical framework for the analysis of the state-labour relation that is based on historical experiences, rather than logically derived from the capitalist mode of production. In so doing I hope to shift the focus from the top-down state-centred theory of the state to a society-centred theory which views the state-labour relation interactive terms. I argue that although the state in capitalist countries may be regarded as capitalist, this is not because the state is determined by the economy, but because the state objectively organises the conditions indispensable to capital accumulation. Liberal capitalism, which is predicated on the autonomisation of politics and the state also creates a space for the working class to struggle for its interests. These struggles, however, take place within the parameters defined for them by the state, as the guarantor of the process of private capital accumulation. Whilst acknowledging the fact that in peripheral capitalist countries, the state is much more involved in the economy than is the case in developed capitalist countries, this involvement must nonetheless be seen in the same light as the state's involvement in the economy anywhere, namely to secure the conditions of production and reproduction of society. What is important are the relations of production under which such process of production and reproduction takes place. Like in developed capitalist countries, the state in peripheral capitalist countries also defines the parameters of working class action. But what the working class can do within those parameters depends on the conjunctural terrain: the international situation, that is the pressures of the international capitalist political economy, the local state, and the strength of organised labour.

Chapter 2 provides a birds's eye view of Botswana for those readers who may not be familiar with the country. Chapter 3 gives an analysis of the class character of the Botswana state and shows that the roots of the present political elite go back to the pre-Independence period. I also give an empirical overview of economic growth and structural transformation that have taken place in Botswana from Independence to 1990. In this chapter I show how the postcolonial state has been in the forefront of economic development through direct investment in infrastructural development and in the establishment of public enterprises. It is argued that these are functions of the state to create the necessary conditions for production and reproduction of the society. The class character of the state and its functions lead to the examination of the form of the Botswana state.

3

Chapter 4 examines the capitalist form of the Botswana state. The form of this state is revealed in the state's relationship to labour. The organising principle of capitalism is the exploitation of wage labour by capital. This exploitation is defined as the ratio of unpaid to paid labour, whereby profits to the capitalists accrue from the surplus value withheld from labour. This system of exploitation of labour has been maintained through a policy of wage restraint which has led to a higher per capita income but to a very unequal income distribution and poverty wages for the workers.

Chapter 5 examines the state's restructuring of the trade union movement and the ideological habituation of the working class. These actions by the state against the working class derive from the state as the disciplinarian of labour on behalf of capital. It is argued that as in other parts of Africa, in Botswana the primary role of state intervention in industrial relations is to restructure and remodel the trade union movement to make organised labour more amenable to state control. The working class has to be habituated to accept the existing exploitative relations of production through the ideology of national interest, etc. It is hoped that in this way, the working class will become supportive or at least acquiescent.

Chapter 6 turns to the examination of labour law in postcolonial Botswana. Habituation is a necessary but not sufficient condition to ensure workers submission to capital. Other structures of control have to be created to ensure that where ideology is insufficient to ensure submission, legal repression will. This chapter demonstrates how Botswana's postcolonial labour laws have weakened the trade union movement organisationally, and disarmed it politically. As it will be shown in the analysis, the state gave with one hand and took away with the other. Whilst the state has created a floor of rights for the workers and a trade union does not have to negotiate for recognition with an employer once it is registered, trade unions have not been allowed to organise in full freedom and workers in the public sector, who comprise a large percentage of the working class in Botswana, are denied the right to form and belong to trade unions. Although collective bargaining is accepted in principle, the employers are not under any legal obligation to disclose information to the workers for the purpose of collective bargaining.

Chapter 7 examines trade union growth and development in postcolonial Botswana. It is pointed out that one of the characteristics of the development of capitalist relations of production is the growth in formal sector employment as labour released from the previously non-wage economic activities are absorbed in formal sector employment in the form of wage labourers. I examine the growth of the working class, disputes settlement and collective bargaining. It is argued that these are integral part of the growth of trade union consciousness.

Chapter 8 examines the working class action within the political and legal parameters imposed by the state and argues that despite these limitations the working class is by no means a hapless and helpless victim of these repressive structures. I show how the working class in Botswana has grown restive, assertive and increasingly militant in its demands and has resorted to illegal strike actions and deliberately disregards laws outlawing strikes. It is argued that these are indicative of the fact that workers are becoming more and more aware of their class position.

Chapter 9 examines the future state-labour relationship in the 1990s and beyond. I point out that restrictions on the labour movement are still in place. This poses new problems for the labour movement. I conclude the analysis by making a case for the need for social movement trade unionism to counteract new forms of labour repression in Botswana. Social movement unionism as distinct from political unionism is the most viable strategic option. I argue that Botswana's liberal democracy, even if just formal, nevertheless creates a political space for the labour movement to form strategic alliances with other democratic organisations and push the state towards more reforms, not only in the industrial relations field, but in society as a whole. It is argued that organised labour remains the most important component of civil society and that its struggles are part of the main struggle for social democracy.

1 Theorising the state-labour relation

Introduction

The empirical analysis that follows next is primarily concerned with the relationship of the state to organised labour in a developing country. It is my contention that this relationship cannot be understood without analysis of the state itself. In most Marxist theories of the state, it has been viewed in terms of its relation to capital rather than labour. The state is often conceived as an instrument that can be wielded by the capitalist class, or more specifically in the case of Third World countries, by the capitalist class in the "centre" together with its allies of the "comprador" or "national" bourgeoisie. These approaches to the state present a top-down theory of the state in which other institutions of civil society, especially the working class, have no effectivity in determining its form. This chapter briefly surveys and critiques some of the Marxist theories of the state with the view of arriving at a more dialectical understanding of the state-society relation and especially the state-labour relation. In highlighting the interactive character of the state and civil society, with specific reference to organised labour, I hope to overcome the division that has been created in the theorisation of the state in developed and developing countries, by highlighting the fact that in both situations it is the imperatives of production relations that shape the behaviour of the state to labour. Secondly, I want to show that whilst the structures of repression, maintained by political power and legitimated by ideology, are real enough, there is always space for struggle within their limits. In other words, organised labour should not be seen as an impotent plaything of the state and capital.

Theorising the modern bourgeois state

My approach to the question of the state is influenced by what I take to be the historical materialist method. My starting point is that the motive force of the

6

development of modern society is the division of society into classes and in particular the struggle between labour and capital. My contention is that the form of the state is determined by the relations between classes and not by the ruling class alone. The form of the state is not predetermined but is decided on the conjunctural terrain, which is a field of objectively possible outcomes of class and political relations in the course of the ongoing struggles.[1]

The starting point is to look at the functions and forms of the state as analytically distinct, though closely related aspects. In a capitalist society the function of the state is to secure the conditions of production and reproduction of the capitalist economy. But how the state organises this process is largely determined by other factors such as the level of the development of productive forces, class formation, class, political and ideological struggles, and the need to balance conflicting interests while at the same time guaranteeing the long term interests of capital accumulation. It is the constellation of these factors which determines the form of the state. Whereas the state intervenes in the social and economic life of the society in which it resides, its form is determined by factors which are independent of its functions. Whilst the state in a capitalist society always acts in a manner that will secure or attempt to secure the long term interests of capital accumulation, this action by the state is circumscribed by the balance of various social forces, not just the interests of the bourgeoisie alone (Fine, 1984; Kelly, 1988). Therefore the state cannot be seen as a mere instrument of class rule.

It is generally agreed that classical Marxism contains a very incomplete analysis of both the state and class. As Jessop (1982) argues, Marx and Engels did not provide any systematic or coherent theory of the state and politics but offered a variety of theoretical perspectives which coexist in an uneasy and unstable union, and their analyses of the state and politics are subsumed under their general critique of political economy of capitalism. However there are certain "key statements" that provide very useful guidelines to be followed in the analysis of the state and its relation to civil society.[2] Marx's key statement appears in a celebrated passage in the *Preface to a Contribution to the Critique of Political Economy,* in which he argued that people enter into social relations that are independent of their will and that these relations are only appropriate to a given stage in the development of the material forces of production. According to Marx (1981), the totality of these relations of production constitutes the economic structure of society, which is the real foundation of society on which arises a legal and political superstructure with corresponding forms of social consciousness.

This statement has attracted a charge of "economic reductionism" because it ultimately reduces the actions of the state, the legal and the political aspects to the requirements of the economy. In a well known statement in the *Communist Manifesto*, Marx and Engels (1968) put it bluntly that the executive of the modern state is but a committee for managing the common affairs of the whole bourgeoisie. The implication here is that at least the executive of the state can be wielded by the capitalist class in pursuit of its own interests. The actions of the state executive are seen to flow directly from the requirements of capital. This formulation seems to suggest that the economic base is self sufficient, that its development is the determinant of social evolution, and that its reproduction does not depend on factors outside its control. But as Jessop (1982, p. 77) points out, to argue that the transformation in the superstructure follows changes in the economic foundations is to imply that political action cannot alter the economic base or even the nature of class relations until economic factors themselves permit or require such alteration.

Engels' key statement on the state appears in *The Origin of the Family, Private Property and the State,* in a passage in which he links the emergence of the state to the inception of private property and the resulting breakdown of a previously "harmonious" communal society. According to Engels (1968a, pp. 586-7), the state is a product of a certain stage of development of society and has arisen to moderate the conflict engendered by opposing economic interests in a class divided society. According to Engels:

> The emergence of the state is the admission that this society has become entangled in an insoluble contradiction with itself, that it has split into irreconcilable antagonisms which it is powerless to dispel. But in order that these antagonisms and classes with conflicting economic interests might not consume themselves and society in fruitless struggle, it became necessary to have a power seemingly standing above society, that would alleviate the conflict, and keep it within the bounds of "order"; this power, arisen out of society, placing itself above it, and alienating itself more and more from it, is the state.

Engels argued further that because the state arose in the midst of the conflict of classes, it is, as a rule:

> ... the state of the most powerful, economically dominant class, which through the medium of the state becomes also the politically dominant class and thus acquires new means of holding down and exploiting the oppressed class ... and the modern representative state is an *instrument* of exploitation of wage labour by capital [emphasis added].

In the passage above Engels argues that the state is "the state of the most powerful, economically dominant class", and that the modern representative state is an "instrument" of the exploitation of wage labour by capital. He also argues that the role of the state is to "alleviate" conflicting economic interests so that the antagonists, the bourgeoisie and the proletariat, do not "consume" themselves and society in an endless struggle. In other words, although the state may be an "instrument" of class rule, how this instrument is actually used, that is, its form, is not something that inheres in the nature of the state, but is determined in the course of the class, political and other forms of struggles. In a letter to J.Bloch, Engels (1968b, pp. 692-3) argued that the charge of reductionism or determinism levelled against him and Marx was misplaced and pointed out that though the determining element in the materialist conception is production and reproduction in real life, that is, in the economic "base" of society, various elements of the superstructure in turn exercise their influence upon the course of the class struggle. He specifically mentions the political forms of the class struggle and argues that although economic conditions are ultimately decisive, political conditions and traditions also play a part in the historical process. According to Badie and Birnham (1983), all the states Marx referred to, like the Prusso-German Empire, Switzerland, England and the United States, had capitalist economic systems but different state forms. Marx viewed the state in the United States as weak and subordinate to civil society; the Prussian state was "nothing but a police guarded military despotism, embellished with parliamentary forms, alloyed with a feudal admixture"; and the French state was dominated by the executive power with its enormous bureaucratic and military organisation, an appalling parasitic body that had enmeshed the body of French society like a net and choked all its pores.

There is therefore present in both Marx and Engels a wide variety of themes and approaches which are capable of independent or even contradictory theoretical developments, but which are combined in various ways in their empirical studies of particular societies and political conjunctures (Jessop, 1982, pp. 9-12). This is due to the different economic and social contexts within which these apparently conflicting theories of the state were articulated. Their "contradictoriness" therefore derives from the fact that Marx and Engels were trying to explain a phenomenon that was spatio-temporal in its materiality. Thus Miliband (1989) argues correctly that what is more useful is not to compare text with text, but text with historical and contemporary reality itself: whether the state is seen as an instrument of class rule, a factor of social cohesion or an institutional ensemble, all are present in the classical works.[3]

The state in the African context

The state in non-European peripheral capitalist societies has not received the same kind of rigorous analysis as it has in developed capitalist countries.[4] In these countries the state has always been analysed against the backdrop of the absence of an economically dominant class, "the bourgeois class", that is, the class that was characterised as the "conquering bourgeoisie", which has captured for itself in the modern representative state, "exclusive political sway" (Marx and Engels, 1968, pp. 35-8). In peripheral capitalist societies, this class exists only in a formative or inchoate form. As a result, it has often been the state, rather than the capitalist class, that has been spearheading the process of economic development in the postcolonial period and has virtually replaced the bourgeoisie (Evans, 1982). Other factors include the complexity and enormous variety of economic and political systems in these countries. In the first place, most of these countries are economically poor and are characterised by extreme inequality in the distribution

9

of wealth and income, high unemployment, debt burdens, inadequate or virtually nonexistent social services (housing, health and education) and backward productive forces.[5] The majority of the people still live in rural areas in subsistence agriculture (Todaro, 1992). Most peripheral capitalist countries are under either a one party system or a military administration, or sometimes even a bit of both. Generally, organisations of civil society such as trade unions, the media and various types of pressure groups are weak as compared to state organs like the army, police and civil bureaucracy.

The analyses of peripheral capitalist societies, especially the neomarxist dependency theory variants, have been conducted on a purely economic terrain, the major preoccupation being to show the effect of international capitalism on peripheral capitalist economies. These factors indicate the difficulties in theorising at a general level the nature and structure of the state and politics in peripheral capitalist societies. Pinkney (1993, p. 2) argues in this vein that:

> It is these social economic circumstances, together with an unequal relationship with the "developed" world outside and in many cases, a recent experience of colonial rule, which help give Third World politics its distinctive flavour, even though there is much diversity between the individual countries.

However, in the last two decades several scholars (notably Alavi, 1972; Ziemann and Lanzendorfer, 1977; Leys, 1976; Beckman, 1981) have made valuable attempts to analyse the state in peripheral capitalist formations. The common thrust of these approaches is twofold: firstly, they reduce the form of the peripheral capitalist state to the requirements of the economic interests of imperialism and its local allies, defined variously as the national bourgeoisie or national comprador class; secondly, these theories are state-centred and ignore the impact of class struggles on the state. Alavi (1972) led the debate in his article on the state in Pakistan and Bangladesh. He argued that the original base of the state in peripheral capitalist countries lay in metropolitan countries and did not rest on the support of any of the indigenous classes; instead it subordinated all indigenous classes to the requirements of metropolitan capitalism. For this reason, he argued, the state in peripheral capitalist societies was "overdeveloped". Alavi advanced two theses: firstly, that the peripheral capitalist countries have inherited an "overdeveloped" state in the form of a huge military bureaucratic machinery; second, and flowing directly from the first, that this overdeveloped state has often pursued its own particular agenda and appropriated a large part of the economic surplus for itself. He argued:

> The apparatus of the state, furthermore assumes also a new and relatively autonomous economic role, which is not parallelled in the classical bourgeoisie state. The state in postcolonial society directly appropriates a very large part of the economic surplus and deploys it in a bureaucratically directed economic activity in the name of promoting economic development. *These are the*

10

conditions which differentiate the postcolonial state fundamentally from the state as analysed in classical Marxist theory (p. 62) [emphasis in the original].

The most sophisticated critique of the peripheral capitalist state theory in general and Alavi's thesis in particular has come from Ziemann and Lanzendorfer (1977). The key point which they make concerns the potentiality of the peripheral capitalist state to promote national economic development. They doubt whether this can be achieved under conditions of peripheral capitalism. In their attempt to go beyond Alavi, Ziemann and Lanzendorfer (1977, p. 155) posit that:

> With the expansion of trade into world trade and the rise of the world market, there has developed, since the days of European colonial expansion, an *international economic system* in which the production and reproduction of all societies in the world are integrated ... With the spread of the dominant reproduction dynamics to world level, the precolonial self centred development of the peripheral societies was blocked, being transformed, in regionally differentiated scope and form depending on the previous historical and natural conditions, into a complementary and subsidiary system attached to the metropolitan system [emphasis added].

According to Ziemann and Lanzendorfer, the condition for the integration of the peripheral capitalist societies into the world market is the imposition on these societies' inner structures of the dominant reproduction dynamics of metropolitan capitalism. The result of this economic relationship is the development of the metropolis and the underdevelopment of the periphery as two sides of a common process, that is, accumulation on a world scale. The independent development of the peripheral societies is blocked, and their inner structure is adapted to the reproductive needs of the metropolis. According to these authors, the peripheral state must be seen as an institution which serves the international economic system. At the economic level the peripheral capitalist state aims at linking the world market with the national economy by breaking down the political frontiers between the world market and the national economy; for example, through its policies on imports and exports, foreign investment and exchange rates. According to Ziemann and Lanzendorfer, the peripheral capitalist state aims at securing the existence and expansion of the world market in the national economic arena, through the reproduction of both internally operating foreign capital and national capital oriented to the world market. To this end, the state guarantees private property rights and repatriation of profits, the extended reproduction of national capital on the home market, infrastructural development, and the reproduction of the labour force. One aspect of this is the state policy by which trade unions are turned into a political instrument for keeping workers on a leash, since their independence could be a barrier to accumulation.

In a similar mode to that of Ziemann and Lanzendorfer, Amin (1987) has argued that the decisive quality that distinguishes the state in the capitalist centre from the state in peripheral capitalism is that in the centre the bourgeois nation-state has crystallised and its essential function is to fulfil the conditions that make possible autocentric accumulation; the state can subordinate external relations to the logic of that accumulation. On the other hand, the peripheral state cannot control local accumulation but is subject to the demands of "globalised accumulation". The direction it takes is determined by the central powers, especially through their instruments of intervention, the World Bank and the International Monetary Fund. Beckman (1981, p. 39) has also argued in this paradigm that the Nigerian state is a comprador state, its institutions and officials operating as agents of imperialism. He argues that:

> The contemporary Nigerian state can ... be described as a comprador state: state institutions and state officials operate as agents of imperialism. The real ruling class is the bourgeoisie of the metropolitan countries. It is not the indigenous businessmen and bureaucrats, who merely masquerade as the "national bourgeoisie". They are allowed to play this role by their foreign paymasters. In fact they are performing a vital ideological function as their nationalist rhetoric conceals the true class nature of the state. When they travel to international conferences attacking "imperialism" and clamouring for a "new international order", they simultaneously take the opportunity to check their international bank accounts which are regularly replenished by their foreign friends.

The basic thrust of this argument is that because the class that has the greatest economic interests is externally based, the Nigerian state is therefore a mere "instrument" of that class and the indigenous capitalist class is a mere conveyor belt of imperialism. Beckman (1981, p. 42) acknowledged that the fact that imperialism "ultimately comes out on top should not allow us to ignore the strength and organisations of the forces which it incorporates, coopts or subdues". These forces and their composition, however, are not analysed; I can only assume that they involve the working class.

The major weakness of all these critics is to repeat this structuralist error in another form: by denying the effectivity of all indigenous social classes and the nation-state itself. In their view, the external pressures of international capitalism make any thought of indigenous accumulation fanciful. It is on the basis of this that I find Alavi's argument more persuasive in that he at least recognises the fact that the state can play an independent role in national economic development of peripheral capitalist societies, and that it has gone some way towards creating viable national economies despite imperial constraints. Ziemann and Lanzendorfer's critique of Alavi is based on a polar opposition: either there has been accumulation or there has not; if there has been accumulation, it is either for national capital or for international capital.

12

In the case of Botswana, attempts to theorise the postcolonial state have been offered by, among others, Pickard (1987) who characterises the Botswana state as an administrative bureaucratic state in which resources are allocated by the bureaucratic elite, authority flows downward from the rulers to the ruled and the bureaucratic elite has complete control over decision making. Pickard (1987, pp. 123-4) argues that the Botswana state is developed at the centre and underdeveloped in the periphery, and that the centralised bureaucracy is a major factor in the policy making process. This bureaucratic state is defined as:

> ... a state of apolitical bureaucratic dominance exercised by an integrated ruling elite of senior civil servants and political leaders that are not controlled by any segment of the population.

In order to theorise empirical situations that do not fit existing conceptual frameworks, a number of ad hoc concepts has been developed to characterise the ruling elite in peripheral capitalist countries. In the African context, Forrest (1987) has identified at least six such concepts: "organisational bourgeoisie", "public sector bourgeoisie", "administrative bourgeoisie", "bureaucratic bourgeoisie" "state bourgeoisie" and "managerial bourgeoisie". All such elites have one thing in common: they are all pursuing capitalist strategies of development. But they may take different political forms, varying from civilian military dictatorship in Pakistan, to military rule in Nigeria, one party rule in Kenya, and liberal democratic capitalism in Botswana. The various forms of state in these countries will affect relations between capital and labour in different ways.

Theorising the state-labour relation

According to some Marxists (notably Althusser, 1971; Altvater, 1978) in developed capitalist countries it is the state that maintains wage labour as an object of exploitation, reproduces general conditions of production (including labour power) and maintains legal relations. According to Althusser:

> The reproduction of labour power requires not only a reproduction of its skills, but also, at the same time, a reproduction of its submission to the rules of the established order, i.e. a reproduction of submission to the ruling ideology for the workers, and a reproduction of the ability to manipulate the ruling ideology correctly for the agents of exploitation and repression, so that they, too, will provide for the domination of the ruling class "in words" (pp. 127-8).

Althusser argues that the state is involved not only in securing the material conditions of production, but also in securing the conditions of the reproduction of relations of production. The latter is ensured in part by the control and

13

manipulation of trade unions. The two are unified in the bourgeois ideology of "national interest", "democracy" and "rule of law". Altvater (1978) argues that there are some social functions that private capital cannot perform because this would imply noncapitalist forms of production, but which are nonetheless crucial for capitalism as a mode of production. In order to secure the overall preconditions of capitalism, the state intervenes in the provision of physical infrastructural development, invests in the fields of education and health, and establishes the legal relations through which relations of legal subjects in capitalist society are mediated. The state also regulates the conflict between wage labour and capital and, if necessary, uses repression against the working class through the law as well as the police and the army. The state also safeguards the existence and the expansion of total national capital on the capitalist world market through its military forces.

The strength of Althusser lies in the fact that his approach to state-labour relations goes beyond simple reductionism or instrumentalism. In particular, he shows that state control of labour is not just repressive but also ideological. His weakness is that his account is too structuralist. He assumes that whatever the state does functions perfectly for capital; he does not give any space to organised labour or class struggle. For example, Althusser (1971, pp. 127-8) argues that the reproduction of labour power consists of learning rules of good behaviour, that is:

> ... the attitude that should be observed by every agent in the division of labour, according to the job he is "destined" for: rules of morality, civic and professional conscience, which actually means rules of respect for the socio-technical division of labour and ultimately the rules of the order established by class domination.

According to this view, therefore, the capitalist state is omnipotent, and the human agents, including organised labour, are impotent automatons manipulated by the state. Altvater does not give labour or class struggle any space either. He also sees state-labour relation in a top-down fashion in which the form of state determines its relationship to labour, rather than the form of the state being determined by the balance of forces in which the labour movement plays a part. However historical experiences tell a different story.

The role the state plays in industrial relations in developed capitalist societies can be properly grasped in the context of concrete historical phases in the development of capitalism. With the advent of the bourgeois revolution, new and different forms of production and reproduction of labour power were required. At the level of social relations this meant the workers could now enjoy certain rights, including the right to enter into contracts of employment with the employer as formally equal legal agents. Formally workers could now work under conditions acceptable to them. At the same time, production requirements ushered in by the factory system made it possible for workers to form trade unions. For example, in Britain, though the state initially curtailed this right by the promulgation of the Combinations Act, the act was repealed in 1875 and in 1906 the British Parliament adopted the Trade

14

Disputes Act. This was not an act of goodwill on the part of the state. These changes were brought about by trade union pressure channelled through the Trade Unions Congress (TUC), which was by then the largest and most powerful in Europe (Kelly, 1988). But even with the repeal of the Combinations Act the British courts still felt impelled by tradition to rest their disapproval of strikes on some formal legal grounds, and pronounced that the united concerted efforts of the workers to refuse to work or challenge conditions of work were a criminal conspiracy to restrain trade (Gregory, 1979). The courts disregarded the statute law and relied on common law, and the workers, who had won a victory over the Combinations Act, were now hemmed in by conspiracy charges.

In the United States, a change in labour law only occurred in 1935 with the adoption of the National Labour Relations Act, commonly known as the Wagner Act. The act initially aroused fierce opposition from the capitalist class which saw it as a concession to the labour movement by the state. The act was even labelled by one newspaper as the most objectionable as well as a "revolutionary" piece of legislation ever presented to Congress that would "out-soviet the Russian soviets" (Klare, 1982). Klare argues that the American capitalists feared that legalising collective bargaining would mean their loss of control over the production process, and that by promoting unionism the act would encourage radicalism and class conflict.

Overtly repressive forms of labour control have gradually been replaced by less repressive forms. The reason is largely due to the growing strength of the working class itself, not the benevolence of the capitalist class or the state. As Zeitlin (1980) argues, the state is the product of the historically specific constellation of class relations and social conflicts in which it is implicated. If it is not to rest on its monopoly of the means of coercion alone, it must incorporate within its structures the interests not only of the dominant but also of the subordinate classes. State policies are therefore impelled by and are the reflection of the struggle between labour and capital for the realisation of their contradictory interests through the state. That is, they are a response to both popular struggles of the subordinate classes and contradictory demands of capital. Thus in the late 1960s advanced capitalist countries were shaken by strike waves which saw two British governments go down in electoral defeat, and in other European countries governments enacted major concessions to restore social order (Kelly, 1988). In France the state introduced the Grenelle Agreement which gave the trade unions the rights to organise at the work place, collect dues and attend training courses without loss of pay, and in Italy, the Labour Statutes were enacted to establish trade union right to organise and hold meetings at the work place. In 1972 the Federal Republic of Germany introduced works councils and granted legal recognition of trade unions at the work place. In 1973 and 1974, the British Government enacted the Work Safety Act and the Security of Employment Act respectively and Sweden enacted the Law on Joint Determination (Kelly, 1988, p. 247).

On the basis of the foregoing examples, it can be argued that though the state in capitalism is not neutral or above class antagonisms, the manner in which particular

15

interests are represented in the state institutions is based on the balance of class forces on the ground. The representation of some interests does not preclude or exclude others. Clarke (1991, pp. 6-9) argues the state has "selective mechanisms" through which to filter the demands placed upon it by various competing interests. What this means is that the state has to carefully balance the interests of capital, namely securing the conditions of sustained accumulation, and avoid compromising its legitimacy by identifying overtly with the interests of any particular class. Within the limits of the need to sustain the accumulation of capital as a whole, the particular policies pursued by the state and the particular interests served by those policies will be contingent on its own political priorities.

Strinati (1979) argues that the form and content of state intervention in the economy is shaped by class struggles mediated through political organisations. According to Strinati, capitalism is predicated upon and distinguished by the institutional separation of the polity and economy. He argues that the capital relation requires the autonomisation of politics and the state from the economy. This autonomy is, however, more apparent than real. Historically, economic processes have been dependent upon specific modes of state intervention, such that these apparently autonomous economic processes have been shaped by conditions of existence that the state actually provides. This does not mean that the state can be regarded as a mere instrument of class rule. Strinati (1979, p. 193) argues that the state is capitalist only insofar as it has structural connections with the capitalist economy and its own internal structures and modes of operation serve to secure the conditions of existence of capital accumulation. He argues:

> The capitalist state is such a state not because it is determined by the capitalist economy but because it objectively organises structures indispensable for the functioning of the capitalist economy: the circuit of capital, the production, realisation and appropriation of the surplus value, generalised commodity production and exchange, the reproduction and restructuring of capital and labour power, the conditions that allow the circuit of capital to exist.

According to Strinati, industrial relations systems reflect forms of state involvement in the economy on an axis from interventionism to *laissez faire*. An industrial relations system should, therefore, be seen not as a hermetically sealed or self sufficient entity, but as a central element in the social structure of capitalism, and in particular it is one of the ways in which class struggles are expressed in capitalist countries.

State-labour relation in the African context

What determines the form and content of state intervention in the African context? What are the options available for the postcolonial state in the struggle for economic development? Whilst the process of economic growth and development may be a goal of all human societies, the strategies adopted to realise this goal are decided at the political level. Most postcolonial governments have chosen a capitalist strategy which emphasises production and economic growth rather than development and social equality, and the belief that production can best be stimulated by the institutions of private property and the market. They stress reliance upon foreign capital and expertise to modernise the economy as well as to encourage indigenous entrepreneurship. The premise is that the goal of economic growth can be achieved through private capital accumulation, with the hope that in the long run the increased output will permit more social welfare and enhanced social justice (Sandbrook, 1975; Sandbrook and Cohen, 1975).

There are two points to note at this juncture. The first is that the adoption of such a strategy of economic management is not a voluntary option but an outcome of indigenous class struggles. Secondly, capitalism is an economic system where the means of production are privately held and where legally free but "capital-less" workers sell their labour power for wages and production decisions are made on the basis of realising surplus value. In a situation where the government has adopted this capitalist strategy, the state now becomes the guarantor of private capital accumulation and private capital accumulation becomes the material base of the state. The mechanisms designed to realise this goal determine its class content. The process of production is geared towards profit maximisation by those who own the means of production and the consequent distribution of social wealth is unequal. Since the state has to maintain this social relationship, this is what influences its relationship to the working class. The state is called upon to regulate class antagonisms, particularly as expressed in the relation between the emergent trade union movements and the requirements of capital accumulation.

This regulation by the state is by no means neutral. In an economic system which emphasises private capital accumulation and private ownership of the means of production, the state will come to depend on those who own the means of production and can sustain the state through taxes and other revenues. Thus when governments in postcolonial Africa treat the trade unions as junior partners in the process of development and restrict the actions of trade unions, this is in order to safeguard the process of capital accumulation and by extension the material base of the state itself (Sandbrook and Cohen, 1975). Since the postcolonial states believe that unrestricted trade unions would adversely affect foreign capital investment and economic growth, the state develops various mechanisms of labour control through which unions can be subordinated to a governmentally defined "national interest". As Sandbrook and Cohen (1975, p. 196) argue:

> The economic justification governments have provided to trammel labour organisation includes charges that the unions' ability to raise wages faster than GNP [gross national product] aggravates inflation, exacerbates balance of payment difficulties, limits the potential rate of economic growth by reducing savings and creates massive urban unemployment by widening urban-rural

differentials, [and that] strike action and worker indiscipline retard productivity and discourage foreign investment.

Gladstone (1978) is in agreement with this perspective. He argues that in a sense the role of trade unions is "preordained": the trade union movement affects the development process and is in turn affected by the way the economy works. What lies at the heart of all this is the industrial relations system. As Gladstone argues, an economy beleaguered by industrial strife cannot perform at its optimum, and a development plan that calls for wage restraint will have a greater chance of success only if the trade unions are supportive or acquiescent. The pivotal role played by the trade unions in the economy has prompted governments to seek to influence, dominate or coopt the trade unions. Gladstone (1979, p. ix) argues that:

> This increased role of the state in industrial relations has taken a number of forms. In certain cases, efforts have been made to rationalise or restructure national trade union movements (and to make them more responsive to the professed national interest) and to influence the choice of leadership. Collective bargaining and agreements in a number of countries have been made subject to approval by official authorities (usually under an official incomes policy aimed at checking inflation and effecting a certain redistribution of national income). Industrial courts or tribunals coupled with compulsory or near compulsory dispute settlement procedures have been instituted.

Kassalow and Damachi (1978) point out that in peripheral societies the functions of trade unions have been defined and redefined according to the perceived needs of national development; in the process trade union freedoms have been restricted and collective bargaining has been "hemmed in" on several sides. Bean (1985, pp. 212-3) also points out that the state in these countries plays a much more active and interventionist role in industrial relations than was traditionally the case in the developed capitalist countries:

> This role is strengthened by the fact that policies are guided by the requirements of national growth oriented development plans and the state itself is much more central to the development process ... Governments in the Third World countries maintain that industrial relations have a direct bearing on the development process since industrial conflict may adversely affect productivity and exports ... Also strikes are not likely to provide a climate which is conducive to the welfare of capital and the attracting of foreign investment.

Bean points out that in peripheral capitalist countries, the process of collective bargaining becomes "trilateral" as opposed to "bilateral" in that wage fixing has to satisfy the objectives not only of management and the unions, but also of the government, because the position of the state as the biggest single employer gives it an additional interest in regulating industrial relations. This has led to the promulgation of restrictive labour laws to control and supervise trade unions or to make them subordinate and acquiescent junior partners. In some cases the policy has been to subordinate the labour movement and "guide" it through legislation towards consensus on the national interest. In such cases legal recognition of trade unions has also been a form of social control in which the labour movement is subjected to all manner of legal rules and regulations. In other words, legal recognition of trade unions and the establishment of procedures for the settlement of disputes not only provide the trade unions with legality, but also with a lesser or greater degree of state control. The aim of legal recognition of trade unions is to orient the trade union movement towards acquiescent and economistic trade unionism rather than political unionism (Gladstone, 1980). These restrictive structures of state control, supervision and regulation of labour, may differ in form but are similar in their objectives: to inculcate capitalist labour discipline and to subordinate labour to capital. This substance cuts across nation states regardless of their political form, be it a military government such as Ghana, a one party civilian dictatorship such as Kenya, a "humanistic" capitalist regime such as Zambia, or a formally liberal democratic regime such as Botswana.[6]

There are three dominant areas of state regulation of labour that can be found in most peripheral capitalist countries in Africa: (a) compulsory registration of trade unions that offers sticks and carrots as conditions of legal acceptance, (b) restructuring and forced amalgamation of trade unions and the creation of central bodies or national centres, sometimes imposed from above, sometimes "voluntary", and (c) the creation of compulsory arbitration procedures to deal with bargaining deadlocks. These forms of labour control stem from the belief by the petty bourgeois state elite that the fragmented nature of trade unions is not conducive to the attainment of a high degree of state regulation and influence and that this can threaten the stability of capital accumulation.

Thus in Ghana, immediately after Independence, the postcolonial state passed an Industrial Relations Act which rationalised union structures by amalgamating house unions into industrial unions, made provisions for a check off system to ensure stable sources of finance for the unions, and compelled the private sector to collectively bargain with the unions (Kraus, 1979). In addition the act created a set of mediation-conciliation-compulsory arbitration procedures to deal with bargaining deadlocks. These procedures made strikes effectively illegal. The powers of the state over unions were significantly increased through the imposition of the secretaries general of the TUC by the state. Kraus points out that the act was maintained by the military government, the National Liberation Council (NLC), which used the act to control workers, arguing that strikes were damaging and wasteful.

In Kenya, after Independence the government moved aggressively to demobilise the trade union movement. According to Sandbrook (1975) the Kenya Federation of Labour (KFL) policy statement in the early 1960s on the role of trade unions in postcolonial Kenya asserted that the trade union movement would remain

19

independent of government and employers, would formulate its own policies and not limit itself only to matters concerning terms and conditions of employment, but would also address questions of human rights, economic policy, housing policy, education and welfare policy. In addition KFL pledged that its own existence as a free and independent movement would be maintained. However, in 1965, two years after Kenya's Independence, the government forced compulsory amalgamation of KFL and the Kenya African Workers' Union (KAWU) to form the Central Organisation of Trade Unions (COTU). COTU came into existence as a result of an official decree by the President. The decree also annulled trade union affiliations to international organisations and provided for the appointment of the general secretary of the national centre from a list of three names submitted to the President. In 1966 a new COTU Constitution was prepared by the Attorney General and imposed on the trade union movement. The Constitution entrenched state supervision of the federation: COTU's governing council, executive board and finance committee had to include government representatives. In 1968, an amendment stipulating that no quorum on the governing council or the executive board would be reached without government representation was added to COTU's Constitution. Iwuji (1979) argues that it was hoped that these measures would contribute not only to the stability of industrial relations, but also to the reinvigorating the economy as whole. Machayo-Omid (1992) argues that the Kenyan government still uses the system of mandatory registration to decide which unions to register, deregister or refuse registration.

Gertzel (1979) argues that since Independence Zambian industrial relations have been characterised by the progressive subordination of the trade union movement to government. The government's control of trade union activity and government intervention in industrial relations has gone hand in hand with formal reaffirmations of the principles of freedom of association and collective bargaining, and in certain circumstances the right to withdraw labour. Gertzel argues that the Industrial Relations Act of 1971, while on the surface giving the employees and employers the right of association and freedom of organisation, greatly extended government control over the trade unions. For example, all unions had to affiliate to the Zambia Congress of Trade Unions (ZCTU), which was given powers over the unions by the state. The act gave effect to government policy of "one industry, one union", laid down procedures for dispute settlement and made conciliation procedures mandatory. Whilst the right of workers to strike was recognised in law, it was significantly restricted by an extensive definition of essential services which covered a much wider area of the economy than basic community needs. The act also stipulated that the legal requirements for settlement of disputes and the mandatory grievances procedures had to be exhausted before any strike action could be taken.

This interference in the affairs of organised labour is not confined to a few African countries, but seems widespread amongst many peripheral capitalist countries. Epstein (1989) argues in the context of Latin America that trade union autonomy has been subjected to considerable pressure from virtually all governments regardless of their particular ideological inspiration. Typical legislation includes regulations concerning the types of workers eligible for trade union membership, the minimum requirements to form officially recognised trade unions, obligations to submit detailed financial records to regular state scrutiny, procedures and conditions for leadership elections, rules for collective bargaining, minimum time limits for engaging in government supervised conciliation of differences, procedures for compulsory arbitration, and conditions under which a legal strike could occur. He argues:

> Democrats and authoritarians; conservatives reformers and radicals; populists and technocratic elite ... all have felt that organised labour occupies too strategic a place in the economy to be allowed unrestricted use of its major means of influence, the threat to strike (p. 276).

What I have described thus far is the manner in which the peripheral capitalist states have sought to control labour movements, usually on the grounds that it is in the interests of the nation to do so. However, these control measures only impose limits on the actions of the trade union movement; they are not in themselves a demonstration of the impossibility of trade union action. Trade union actions of various sorts are still possible even within the limits of these state restrictions, and sometimes the labour movement develops its own counter ideologies to resist or defy the authority of the state. Labour control and labour resistance comprise the dialectic of structure and action.

The challenges of the labour movement

Chenge (1987) has calculated that in Kenya between 1974 and 1983, some 363,444 days were lost to industry due to strike actions. According to Chenge, most of the strikes were about pay. Chenge argues that although there is a positive correlation between declining real wages and strike activity, the strikes did not solely arise from falling real wages, but included such factors such as violation of conditions of service, unfair dismissals, poor industrial relations and racism on the part of management. According to Chenge, strike days lost were due to both prolonged strikes in a few industries and nationwide general strikes lasting short periods. In 1974, which saw a record 127,951 days lost, 50 per cent of the strike days were accounted for by the white collar Bank Workers' Union. In 1978, 72 two per cent of the strike days were accounted for by the largely multinational dominated manufacturing industry, and in 1981, 61 per cent of the strike days were lost to the agricultural sector. The general tendency of Kenyan strikes, Chenge argues, is that they involved white collar workers, perhaps demonstrating that it is the more educated workers who are most strike prone.

In Zambia, Liato (1989) argues that different perceptions and expectations of what independence promised to deliver, and the divergent interpretations of the role of trade unions in an independent state, led to conflicts between the ruling party and the trade union leadership, which has since the 1970s been made up of "economistically" oriented leaders. This cadre of leaders placed emphasis on the economic interests of workers and on the need for the trade union movement to maintain its organisational autonomy. Heightened tension between labour and the state induced both further incorporative efforts by the state and restiveness on the part of the trade union rank and file, undermining the strategy of worker acquiescence.

According to Liato, there was an average of 109 strikes a year between 1966 and 1985. Between 1966 and 1983, the agricultural sector, which employed 9.43 per cent of the Zambian work force accounted for 8.64 per cent of strike actions; the manufacturing sector, with 11.74 per cent of employment, had the highest number of strikes, accounting for 32.07 per cent of the total. The mining sector, which employed 15.92 per cent of the work force accounted for 12.61 per cent of the strike activities. She points out that between 1980 and 1985, there was a total of 495 strikes, with a total of 809,201 strike days lost to industry. Most of the strikes were of an economic nature, motivated by disputes over wages. Other strikes were caused by grievances related to economic issues such as disputes over collective labour agreements, unfair dismissals, unfair labour practices by management, and the use of insulting or abusive language.

These challenges to capital by the working class need to be situated in the broader perspective of state-labour relation. There are two central issues that characterise this relation: those of labour control and labour resistance. Labour control refers to the activities of the representatives of capital to assert authority over labour and thereby incorporate it into capitalist relations of production. Labour resistance refers to the activities of representatives of labour to defy the authority of capital, assert the autonomy of labour and obstruct its incorporation into capitalist relations of production (Crisp, 1984, pp. 1-6).

According to Crisp, capital seeks to maximise surplus value appropriation by habituating workers to the unequal distribution of the product of their labour and to the unequal distribution of effort and authority in the work place. In order to achieve these objectives, capital will seek to minimise the resistance of the workers by controlling their political activity. To protect capital and safeguard its privileged status, the state elite is able to use a wide range of legislative measures to obstruct the unionisation of workers and restrict the financial and administrative autonomy of established unions.

Workers also use a variety of methods to confront capital and the state. The methods of resistance can be informal, collective or institutional: they include familiar ones such as strikes and go-slow, and less familiar and less visible ones like malingering, absenteeism, theft, sabotage and restricted output. Workers respond to strategies of control imposed on them by taking their own initiatives, shifting between modes of resistance and forcing capital and the state to respond with new strategies of control.

Conclusion: towards a theoretical framework

The foregoing analysis reveals the state-labour relation as interactive and not top-down. Whilst it is generally agreed that in capitalist countries there is a fundamental structural connection between the state and the capitalist economy and that the state creates conditions that are indispensable to the process of capitalist accumulation, how this process unfolds is, however, is decided on the conjunctural terrain. Both the capitalist class and the working class make demands on the state. These demands are by no means evenly represented, but since the state cannot use coercion all the time, it is forced to make concessions to the working class. These concessions point to two issues. Firstly, the state is institutionally separate from the economy, and has its own identity. But because of the structural connections between the state and the capitalist economy, the state is not neutral. Secondly, there is a need to balance the conflicting interests in society. This "balancing act" is carried out within the parameters of attempts to secure the long term interests of private capital accumulation in order to perpetuate the capitalist mode of production.

The parameters of this process are not defined by the state alone, in whichever way it likes, but are a result of class struggles and compromises. In its intervention, the state has to take account of the balance of class and political forces at any one point of time, reflecting the need for the state to continually readjust its position in order to maintain its hegemony and the cohesion of the social formation. Hegemony is maintained not by coercion alone but also by securing the consent of the dominated class by means of political and ideological domination to the extent that particular interests of the capitalist classes are successfully presented as the general interests of all. This involves taking systematic account of popular interests and demands, shifting position and making compromises on secondary issues to maintain support and alliances in an inherently unstable and fragile system of political relations, and organising support for the attainment of national goals which serve the fundamental long term interests of the dominant class (Jessop, 1990). The state-society relation in general, and the state-labour relation in particular make the state a complex entity which cannot just be regarded as an instrument of the bourgeoisie. Historical materialist analysis does not focus on the structures of repression alone, which undoubtedly impose limits, but also on the tactics, strategies and actions of the working class and other social forces. This is the task to which I turn in the chapters that follow.

Notes

1   Imperialism and cold war rivalry have been very crucial factors in peripheral capitalism. Imperialism has always intervened militarily, politically and at an ideological level on the side of the peripheral capitalist state to defeat working class struggles. However, these defeats do not

always end in surrender. The working classes of peripheral capitalist societies continue to engage their class opponents in the ongoing struggles for better conditions of service and a more equitable distribution of social wealth, even if these struggles are carried within the framework of the existing exploitative social relations.

2   For an extended discussion of these guidelines refer to Jessop (1982, Chapter 5).

3   Jessop (1990) identifies six approaches to a Marxist theory of the state: (a) the state as a parasitic institution that plays no essential role in economics production or reproduction, (b) the state as an epiphenomenon of the system of property relations and the resulting class struggle, (c) the state as a factor of social cohesion regulating class conflicts in the interests of the dominant class, (d) the state as an instrument of class rule which can be captured by the dominant class, (e) the state as a set of institutions, and (f) the state as a system of political domination with specific effects on the class struggle.

4   I use the terms "peripheral capitalism", "Third World" and "developing countries" interchangeably to refer to all countries that are outside Europe and North America. Most of these countries are located in Africa (excluding South Africa), Asia (excluding the so called newly industrialised countries of Singapore, Hong Kong, Taiwan and South Korea) and in Latin America. I follow the accepted United Nations usage of these terms and do not accept the pejorative meanings that have been attributed to these by the Western press.

5   The meaning of economic development is by no means uncontestable. My definition of economic development follows closely therefore the definition given by Todaro (1989).

6   However, research from other parts of Africa shows that the state regulation of labour is not new and that there are discernible continuities with labour policies from the colonial period (Damachi, U.G. et al., 1979; Iwuji, 1979; Freund, 1988; Gertzel, 1979; Sandbrook, 1975).

2 Botswana: an overview and rapid assessment

Introduction

Botswana lies at the heart of the southern African subcontinent. The country is completely landlocked, being surrounded by South Africa in the south, Zimbabwe in the east, and Namibia in the west and north-west. Physically, Botswana is a very large country. Its total land area is 582,000 square kilometres, about the size of France, or the state of Texas in the USA. However, Botswana's huge physical size is out of proportion to its population. The 1991 population census put Botswana's population at 1,326,796. Of this, 1,010,154 people were living in the rural areas, and only 316,642 lived in Botswana's four major urban areas. Gaborone, the capital city, had some 133,468 people, or more than a third of Botswana's urban population.[1] Although Botswana can boast about the Okavango Delta, the biggest inland drainage system in the world, which also has the most varied species of flora and fauna, most of the country is flat and dry. More than two thirds of the land area are covered with the thick sand layers of the Kgalagadi Desert. Most *Batswana* live in the eastern region of the country, where soils are more fertile.[2]

Colonial economic legacy

Botswana was colonised by Britain in the mid 1880s, but for the entire colonial period the country remained undeveloped, and was used mainly as a labour reserve colony for South Africa. At the time of Independence (from Britain, in 1966), Botswana was listed amongst the world's poorest countries. It was uncharitably labelled a "hopeless basket case" (Colclough and McCarthy, 1980). Botswana was so lowly rated by the Colonial Office that the country was even ruled from outside its borders, from Mafikeng in the Cape Colony: the only case in the annals of the history of British imperialism. As Harvey and Lewis (1990) point out, the country

25

suffered social and economic neglect, even by the standards of colonial Africa. The authors point out:

> Despite more than 80 years of British rule, Botswana inherited very little in 1966: very little infrastructure, and very few people with education, training, or experience except that provided by traditional activities and low level work in South African mines and farms ... until before Independence, ... the country had no capital city, nor even the benefits of the small spending power of the colonial administration. Another symbol of neglect was that the Bechuanaland Protectorate never had its own governor like other colonies; the governor was the British high commissioner to the Cape Colony, and later to the Union of South Africa (p. 15).

Botswana must rank as one of the few countries in the world that never benefited even indirectly from the industrial revolution that changed the face of the world, especially Europe and North America. Botswana inherited very little in terms of social and economic infrastructure from the colonial period. The developments that were bequeathed from the colonial period included a single track railway line built by the British South Africa Company to link the Cape Colony with Southern Rhodesia. There were very few economic activities outside pastoral and arable farming. Manufacturing industry was almost nonexistent, and there was no viable indigenous capitalist sector. Commercial activities consisted of a creamery, and a bonemeal and animal fodder plant in Francistown and an abattoir, a maize and malt mill in Lobatse, and small shops scattered around the country. Other commercial activities like wholesale and retail business activities were few and far between and were controlled by foreigners (Harvey and Lewis, 1990).

The situation was even more hopeless in relation to human resources. In a population of about 549,000 at Independence, there were only 71,546 children in primary schools, and 1,531 in secondary schools. There were only nine secondary schools with only two offering O'level examinations. Of the only 43 secondary school teachers with university education, just six were *Batswana*. The country was believed to have about 100 people with a secondary school leaving certificate. At Independence, Botswana had only 20 km of bitumen road. The rest of the road network, about 7,000 km long, was just dirt tracks. The budget at Independence in 1966 was P13m, but revenues were only P6m, and Britain had to provide grants in aid, to balance the budget and pay civil servants salaries.[3] Compared to the other so called High Commission Territories of Lesotho and Swaziland, Botswana was worse off, in the sense that these countries could at least boast of a modicum of commercial activities that were taking place in and around their administrative headquarters.

A question may be posed as to why Botswana was treated so differently by Britain, and why no efforts were made to develop minimum infrastructure. According to Colclough and McCarthy (1980), Botswana differed from the classical type of a colony in the sense that Britain was not attracted to Botswana by the availability of raw materials and other economic resources that could be exploited, but because of military and strategic considerations. Halpern (1965a) points out that the strategic importance of Botswana lay in its being what Cecil Rhodes called the "Suez Canal to the North". Inside South Africa, Britain was facing rebellious Boers. In fact Britain had just been defeated by the Boers in the first Anglo-Boer War in 1880. Externally, Britain was also facing military challenge and feared that the Germans in South West Africa (Namibia), the Portuguese in Mozambique, and the land hungry Boers who had already annexed the southern part of Botswana, might between them annex the central part of Southern Africa and close the British route from its base in the Cape Colony to Central Africa. On 30 September 1885, Britain instructed the commander of its expeditionary force in the Cape Colony, Sir Charles Warren to extend British presence to latitude 22^0 South. According to Halpern, the colonisation of Botswana was therefore to secure Botswana as a link to Cairo in an unbroken imperial line.

Because of its economic unattractiveness, Botswana remained just a buffer zone between the Germans and the Boers and no industrial or commercial activities were encouraged. Colclough and McCarthy (1980) argue that the British attitude was to keep the financial cost of their involvement in Botswana to a minimum. The governor of the Cape Colony is reported as having said that the British Government would do "as little in the way of administration or settlement as possible" (Colclough and McCarthy, 1980, p. 12). In order to generate revenue for administering the country from local sources, the colonial administration introduced a "hut tax" system that was administered by the chiefs, who were given ten per cent for their responsibilities.

Although Botswana was supposed to be a "protectorate", and not a "colony" in the classical sense, some of the actions by Britain in its relations to the local political structures did not differ from the actions of a colonialist state in a classical colony. For example in 1890 Britain divided up the country and redesignated the fertile parts of Botswana like the Tuli Block, the Molopo Farms, Gaborone and Lobatse into the so called "Crown Lands", and demarcated "tribal reserves" for the indigenous people (Colclough and McCarthy, 1980). In 1934, Britain introduced the Native Administration Proclamation to curtail the juridical powers of the chiefs and gave the colonial state authorities the power to suspend chiefs if they were not performing their duties satisfactorily (Crowder, 1988). In 1954 Britain banned Seretse Khama from returning to Botswana after he married a white Briton. The ostensible reason given was that Seretse Khama's wife was not acceptable to his own people and that this might cause "tribal animosity". However, it has emerged that the British Government was under pressure from the apartheid government in South Africa which regarded the Khama marriage as bad example (Dutfield, 1990).

Other colonial state actions included the Credit Sales to Natives Proclamation (1923) which restricted the borrowing capacity of *Batswana* to £35 a year, restricted Batswana's economic activity to agriculture, and reserved modern commercial activities for Europeans and Indians only.[4] The absence of any industrial or manufacturing base resulted in the establishment of a nationwide

27

migrant labour recruitment network after the introduction of the hut tax by the colonial state. As a result of this, many able bodied young men, especially from poor families who could not produce surplus to meet their tax obligations, were forced to go and make a living in the South African mines. The migrant labour system became a major source of wage employment in colonial Botswana.

At the time of Independence, about 30 per cent of *Batswana* between the age of 20 and 40 were working in South African mines, manufacturing industries and farms or as domestic labourers (Harvey and Lewis, 1990; NDP 7, p. 11). But the migrant labour system, which was organised on a contract basis of 6 to 12 months, could not support trade union activity in the territory. The work place and the home of the "contract" worker were geographically separated, and this section of the working class remained in disarray. In any case apartheid laws in South Africa did not allow black workers to form trade unions. This remained the situation until 1965 when Botswana was granted self government. Independence came on 30 September 1966.

Postcolonial developments

Since Independence the country has undergone rapid economic transformation. There have been significant changes in the country's social, economic and physical landscape. Important indicators of these structural changes include the growth of formal sector employment, urbanisation, the building of good roads and telecommunications network, the creation of an educational and health infrastructure, and an improved standard of living for most people, especially those in urban areas (Harvey and Lewis, 1990; NDP 7, p. 11). In 1996, Botswana's per capita income was about P8,000 (US$3,000), foreign reserves stood at P13 billion and the total budget was about P6 billion. This economic performance has triggered numerous positive commentaries about Botswana. Some economists have characterised Botswana as an African, and sometimes even as a Third World economic success story, alongside the so called Asian tigers of Taiwan, Korea and Singapore (Lewis and Sharpley, 1988; Harvey and Lewis, 1990). Some political scientists (Good, 1992) have described Botswana as a shining example of liberal democracy in a continent notorious for one party states and military dictatorship. The most recent of these glowing commentaries on Botswana has come from Stedman (1993, p. 1) who argues that:

> At a time when Africa's dismal economic performance and political corruption and mismanagement have given rise to a new intellectual movement called "afropessimism", when analysts create generic models of African governments that include "lame leviathans", "swollen states", "kleptocracies", and "vampire states", Botswana stands out as an example of economic development, functioning governance, multiparty liberal democracy. It is ... a country akin to Switzerland, an exception that confounds generalisations, but whose very

exceptionality prompts analysts to see it as a hopeful model for other societies.[5]

Stedman, like Harvey and Lewis (1990) then goes on to give a description of Botswana's economic growth, increase in per capita income and growth in the gross domestic product (GDP), growth in formal sector employment, investment in social infrastructural development in areas such as health, education and rural water supply, and drought relief and drought recovery programmes as examples of how the benefits of rapid economic growth were distributed throughout the society. Harvey and Lewis also point out that between 1974 and 1986 formal sector employment has increased by 150 per cent while the population has increased by only 65 per cent, and that this was a major gain in welfare because even rural households benefited from the growth of employment through remittances from household members with urban jobs. They also cite as an example of the benefits of rapid economic growth the fact that only a small number of *Batswana* are still going to South Africa from employment. They argue that rural households gained not just from the absolute increase in the opportunity to get employment, but from a shift in the composition of job opportunities to working in Botswana rather than under the conditions of apartheid.

My dissatisfaction with all these commentaries is that they are partial, tendentious and look at Botswana superficially. They have looked at economic growth and structural transformation as if these processes take place in a vacuum, and have left out the analysis of the relations of production that are inscribed in the process. Class formation is simply referred to as employment creation, the repressive state policies that have been created to control the working class have been ignored and the state is rewarded with praise. For example, whilst I acknowledge the empirical facts concerning economic growth and structural transformations, my argument is that in fact it is the function of the state to secure the production and reproduction of the society. The postcolonial state's involvement in the economy must be seen within this context. It is not as if the Botswana state was doing the society a favour by its interventionist policies of creating the necessary infrastructure. The new dimension that I raise in this study is to draw attention to the class contradictions that have emerged.

My argument is that in a class divided society, where private capital accumulation is seen as the best way of securing social production and reproduction, class contradictions inevitably arise because the relations of production embedded in this process are conflictual. The development path adopted by the postcolonial state, and the state's reliance on private capital accumulation, necessitate the political control of the working class. To this end the state creates structures of repression in order to trammel organised labour. However, as both the economy and organised labour grow quantitatively and qualitatively, these structures will be challenged by the working class.

29

State-society relations in Botswana

Freund (1988, p. 95) points out that Botswana is a country unusual in its tolerance of autonomous civil institutions by African standards. As we shall see in the chapters that follow, such characterisation of the Botswana state is too generous. It is true that unlike most independent African countries, Botswana has continued to adhere to a liberal democratic constitution inherited at Independence. Elections have been held regularly at five year intervals since 1965. The postcolonial state has allowed for the existence of a multiparty system. There are about ten registered political parties, although only two parties, the ruling Botswana Democratic Party (BDP), and the main opposition, the Botswana National Front (BNF) are taken seriously. The BDP has 27 seats and the BNF has 13 seats in a parliament of 40 seats. If all goes well, Botswana will go to the polls again in 1999 for the eighth time since Independence.[6] The state-society relation in Botswana is, however, a complex mixture of repression, corporatism and paternalism. This itself is the result of a combination of several factors, including a liberal democratic constitution that guarantees fundamental human rights and freedoms, and the populist nationalism of the BDP, which, although a strong advocate of capitalism, has been able to maintain its hegemony on Botswana's body politics. But as some commentators on Botswana like Molutsi and Holm (1990, p. 327) have pointed out:

> Government is assuming some corporatist characteristics: policy initiation takes place within government ministries; persuasion is presented as consultation; limits are placed on participation in politics; government dominates communication processes, and ministries create and control most organised groups.

Molutsi and Holm further point out that the government restricts political communication through its hold on Radio Botswana and proposals for private radio stations have been rejected; the official media avoids politically controversial issues, while the private newspapers are hamstrung by fear of financial and legal sanctions by the government or those associated with the ruling party. The idea that organs of civil society should lobby political parties and form alliances is officially discouraged, even though not prohibited by law, and the term "politics" refers only to the activities of political parties, while pressure groups, such as trade unions, are expected to take their problems to public officers rather than lobby politicians and seek to influence government action directly (Molutsi and Holm, 1990). The researchers who have so fulsomely praised Botswana's liberal democracy and successful capitalist development have to a large extent ignored these issues. To me this is a serious omission and a gap in knowledge that has to be rectified. The postcolonial state's relationship with the labour movement forms part of the picture that has not yet been critically analysed. What is often ignored in most analyses about Botswana is that the attainment of independence left the postcolonial state with an urgent need for accelerated economic development. Like most Third World

30

countries, Botswana could only achieve this by creating repressive structures, at both political and ideological levels, to control the trade union movement and make it acquiescent or supportive. However, much as the state tries to repress, regulate and dominate labour on behalf of capital, labour also puts up its resistance to such repression, regulation and domination. The working class, by its demands and resistance to certain forms of labour control, affect state policies, and forces the state to formulate new policies. In this regard, Clark and Dear (1984, p. 4) point out that though the state maintains the capitalist system, the state is not the exclusive domain of the capitalists, but interacts with society in a continuous spiral of responses and counter responses which in turn move the society toward some further development, generating new difficulties and leading yet to a further round of state intervention.

Notes

1   See the *Report on Population and Housing Census*, Central Statistics Office, Ministry of Finance and Development Planning: Gaborone.

2   A citizen of Botswana is *Motswana* (*Batswana* is the plural form). *Setswana* is the national language. The word *Tswana* is used interchangeably with the full form *Setswana* to denote ethno-cultural descent.

3   *Pula* (P) is the monetary unit of Botswana, equal to 100 *thebe*.

4   See the *Bechuanaland Protectorate Credit Sales to Natives Proclamation*, No. 38 (1923), Her Majesty's Stationery Office: London.

5   In 1992, some ministers were implicated in corruption by the Kgabo Commission on land allocations in peri-urban areas and by the Christie Report on the operations of the Botswana Housing Corporation. Peter Mmusi, the country's vice president and national chairman of the ruling Botswana Democratic Party, Daniel Kwelagobe, Secretary General of the party and Minister of Agriculture, and Ronald Sebego, assistant minister in local government, were forced to resign. Michael Tshipinare, another assistant minister in local government, was fired from the cabinet and served a term of imprisonment for receiving a bribe of P500,000. Joe Letsholo, the late manager of the Botswana Housing Corporation, was said to have kept close to P250,000 in a safe in his office. The Christie Commission also alleged that the deceased had in a very short time built an estate of over P3m.

6   I use the concept of liberal democracy with caution, because although the constitution of the country has all the outside trappings of liberal democracy, what happens on the ground is quite different. I will give only three examples. First, the ruling party monopolises the use of state resources like Radio Botswana and *The Botswana Daily News*, which are

being used as party and state organs of persuasion with BDP political broadcasts being presented as government "consultation". Airtime for the opposition is minimal and there is always a risk that opposition party broadcasts can be taken off the air by a simple ministerial instruction to the radio station, which is staffed by civil servants. Foreign journalists have been expelled under a presidential decree. Secondly, the Botswana state machinery is centralised in a top heavy bureaucracy based in Gaborone (especially in the Office of the President, which has all the executive powers), with several line ministries, such as the Ministry of Local Government and Lands, which is responsible for local authorities and for the implementation of projects and programmes. Since the opposition party started winning the urban councils, the government has resorted to a policy of cutting down financial grants to local authorities or councils that are under the control of the opposition - a practice that shows that the electorate is being penalised for voting opposition parties. Thirdly, the ruling party has always "specially elected" councillors and parliamentarians, usually people who have been unsuccessful in the elections, to increase the number of BDP representatives and overturn the opposition majority.

3 The Botswana state in historical perspective

Introduction

In a capitalist system the means of production are privately owned and private capital accumulation is regarded as the most effective way of generating the society's material wealth. The state, which relies on corporate taxes and other revenues provided by private capital, serves to secure the interests of private capital accumulation. The state assists in securing the conditions of capital accumulation by performing functions which private capital cannot or will not meet but which are nonetheless vital for capitalism as a mode of production. These functions include infrastructural development and the reproduction of labour through the provision of basic education, training, health care and general social welfare. The state also assists private capital accumulation through fiscal and monetary policies and state regulation and political and ideological domination of labour. The object of this chapter is to analyse the manner in which the postcolonial state in Botswana, a society with its own historical and social and economic peculiarities, has set about this task. The chapter starts first by examining the historical emergence of the postcolonial Botswana state and reveals how the roots of the petty bourgeois elite that controls the Botswana state go back to the precolonial period. This is followed by an empirical analysis of the economic growth and structural transformation of the political economy of Botswana in the postcolonial period, a process that was spearheaded by the new state elite. It is argued that by investing in infrastructural development, the modernising elite which controls the Botswana state was performing a necessary function vital for the reproduction of the capitalist system.

It is true that some economic growth has indeed taken place in Botswana since Independence. There has been an increase in economic output measured in terms of gross domestic product and income per capita. However, this growth was marked by uneven development. Some sectors of the economy grew faster than others, and other sectors like agriculture experienced decline both in relative and in absolute terms. Some people's wealth and power have increased while the majority of the people's wealth and power have declined. The development process in Botswana was accompanied by a particular process of class formation and class contradictions. As in most capitalist countries, the intervention of the Botswana state in the economy was not exceptional. What was important were the specific relations of production that characterised this process. It is necessary to start this analysis with the examination of the character of the present Botswana state because the character of the state gives vital clues about its functions and policies.

The class character of the Botswana state

Botswana was a class divided society even before the advent of colonialism. The traditional *Tswana* social structure was organised on a system of *merafe* or nations, each with its own *kgosi* or king who was patrilineally descended from the *morafe's* founder. Social differentiation was based on both economic position and status. At the top of the social hierarchy was the *kgosi* and his closest relatives. These made up the royal household. After this came the layer of *dikgosana* or the aristocracy. This layer was made up of the king's other relatives like uncles and cousins. The third layer was that of *sechaba*, that is, commoners or ordinary people. Below the layer of the commoners was that of *bafaladi* or immigrants, and below the layer of immigrants were *batlhanka* or hereditary serfs. All of these classes had different privileges and obligations.[1]

The highest organ of the state was the *kgotla* or village assembly, presided over by the king, who was a "presidential monarch" (Crowder, 1988, p. 22). The *kgotla* made all political, administrative and judicial decisions. The king exercised his powers through a hierarchy of relatives, close advisers and headmen, whose authority was exercised within *dikgotlana* (ward assemblies). These were specific geographical spaces which resembled boroughs or wards but which were inhabited by related households within the village (Parson, 1984). These boroughs or wards were the lowest organs of the state and could also make political, administrative and judicial decisions, subject to approval by the *kgosi* and the *kgotla*. In principle every adult male had the right to make a contribution to the deliberations at the *kgotla*. However, in practice the *kgotla* was dominated by a few members of the royal family, the aristocracy and the king's advisers. These men were also substantial cattle owners who because of their wealth had considerable political influence. The actual level of participation in the debates at the *kgotla* was subject to wealth, status and the ability to articulate thoughts (Gossett, 1986, p. 103).

There is a famous proverb in Botswana which says *kgosi ke kgosi ka batho,* that is, the king rules by (the will of) the people. The *kgotla* was therefore also used by the *kgosi* to gauge the public mood and popular sentiments. Although the king had "executive powers", and the advise of the *kgotla* was not binding, to ignore it would be unwise and a calculated risk which at times led to the assassination or banishment of the *kgosi* (Gossett, 1986). As Gossett further points out, at the same time the king was only too aware of the potential threat posed by other members of the royalty or the aristocracy, who were in the line of succession and could possibly challenge the king for his position. Parsons (1993, p. 115) has recorded some seven coups and counter coups in the Bamangwato territory between 1834 and 1875.

Although Botswana was a part of the British empire, British interests were primarily in Central and South Africa, and the country was not viewed as being of primary importance. According to Parson (1984), Botswana had to be self supporting and not to become a permanent ward of the British treasury; in order to meet the administrative costs locally, the colonial state imposed the hut tax. The British introduced what was called "parallel rule", a form of indirect rule based on the assumption that Botswana was being "protected from external threat" posed by the Boers and the Germans, and that the British administration would have no effect in the internal affairs of the country. According to Pickard (1985, p. 11) the basic principle of the system of parallel rule was that:

> The European administration would exist to regulate the affairs of traders, missionaries and other Europeans in the district, and the magistrates would mediate in terms of the relations between the chiefs and the outside world.

However, this principle seems to have been honoured more in breach than in observance. Ever since 1891, the colonial administration created structures to help it govern the colony effectively. In 1919 it created the Native Advisory Council, which was a forum for all the Batswana's *dikgosi* (the monarchs) and some specially appointed councillors. In 1920 the colonial state created the European Advisory Council to represent the interests of the 2,000 white traders in the "tribal reserves" and farmers in the freehold farming blocks such as the Tuli Block and Molopo. In 1950 the colonial administration created a Joint Advisory Council.

These councils lacked legislative powers and were used mainly as forums for the colonial administration to announce its plans. The Native Advisory Council was especially used to try to persuade the traditional leaders to accept their subordinate role (Parson, 1984). The colonial administration plan to gradually take away the powers of the traditional leaders reached its climax in the 1930s, when Charles Rey promulgated the Native Administration Proclamation and Native Tribunals Proclamation. The Native Administration Proclamation established tribal councils to "advise" each *kgosi* on the affairs of the society. The Native Tribunals Proclamation sought to remove the judicial powers of the *kgotla* and create a system of "tribunals" in which the *kgosi* would now be assisted by only two assessors. These two proclamations were fiercely opposed by the traditional leaders who realised that they were about to lose power, as they would no longer be the final arbiters of matters political, administrative and judicial (Crowder, 1988).

There were two factors that were crucial to the development of nationalist politics in Botswana later. The first concerned the relationship of some members of the traditional aristocracies to the colonial administration and the second concerned the relationship of the aristocracies to *dikgosi*. The *Tswana* aristocracies were made up of men who were substantial cattle owners. Because of their wealth, they were also relatively educated people, some with matriculation, and one, Kgalemang Motsete, had three degrees - a BA, a BD, and a BMus from the University of London (Halpern, 1965b). Motsete, as we shall see later, was undoubtedly the most educated man in Botswana at that time, and after the 1950s played a very crucial role in nationalist politics. One of his final but abiding contribution to Botswana's nationalism was to compose Botswana's republican national anthem, *Fatshe Leno La Rona*, whose English translation is "This Land is Ours".

At the same time that the colonial administration was trying to curb the powers of the traditional rulers, it also antagonised this group of the aristocracy. First, through the Credit Sales to Natives Proclamation of 1923, which was ostensibly to protect *Batswana* against cheating by some unscrupulous white traders, but had the effect of restricting *Batswana* from engaging in commerce. The proclamation restricted the emergence of the indigenous commercial sector so much that as late as 1949 there were only ten shops owned by *Batswana*, as opposed to the 155 European owned shops (Parson, 1984).[2] Secondly, in 1924, a glut in the South African beef market pushed down producer prices of white South African farmers. The South African Government imposed a trade embargo in the form of weight restrictions on the importation of cattle from Botswana to South Africa. This trade embargo denied the *Tswana* aristocracy, which owned large herds of cattle, access to beef markets and also affected their capacity to accumulate. These types of economic pressure were important ingredients in the growth of the *Tswana* nationalism.

Although this group was made up of men of aristocratic or royal background, with wealth and good education, some of them were not in a position of power and influence within the traditional political structure. Although they were not happy with the colonial administration's position regarding African commerce and trade, they seemed quite prepared to collaborate with the colonial administration to curtail the powers of the traditional rulers (Crowder, 1988). According to Crowder some of these men supported the colonial state in its endeavours to curb the powers of the traditional leaders whom they saw as autocratic and feudal. They also gravitated more towards a kind of "bourgeois nationalism" and wanted the country to move towards a western type of parliament (Pickard, 1985). Crowder (1988, p. 47) argues that like the educated elite elsewhere in Africa, the elite in Botswana "resented the power of the traditional rulers and saw itself, rather than these heirs to the past, as the future leaders of their people".

This group, however, remained politically unorganised until the early 1960s when they coalesced into a political party, the BDP. The manner in which this group emerged is of interest because it was in this group that the colonial state found local allies against the radical nationalist Botswana People's Party (BPP). The BDP came about as a reaction to the emergence of the BPP which was formed in the aftermath of the banning of black political organisations in South Africa - including the African National Congress (ANC), the Pan Africanist Congress (PAC) and the multiracial Communist Party of South Africa. The BPP was formed by a group of radical nationalists, some of whom had been political activists in South Africa before the banning. The BPP demanded early independence, africanisation of the civil service and nationalisation of the land. According to Halpern (1965b, p. 287), the BPP was also strongly antitribalist and critical of chieftainship, which it referred to as a "an ancient institution" that had no place in present day Botswana. It denounced tribalism as a form of "communal chauvinism" characterised by "belief in a mythical hereditary divine right of precedence" and demanded that political office should be based on merit alone.

The main players were K.T. Motsete, who was the president of the party, Philip Matante, the vice president, and Motsamai Mpho, the secretary general. The BPP was, however, an uneasy alliance. Soon the ideological differences that had led to the split in the black opposition politics in South Africa and to the creation of the PAC, were reproduced within the BPP (Gossett, 1986). According to Gossett, the internal dispute in the BPP concerned mainly two issues. First, there was an anticommunist pro-PAC faction led by Philip Matante, and a pro-ANC faction led by Motsamai Mpho. The pro-PAC faction, with the support of some PAC elements, started accusing the pro-ANC faction of being a front for (white) communists, and its leader Motsamai Mpho, of being a communist agent. Secondly, at about the same time that these allegations were going on, some monies donated by the Africa support groups based in Ghana went missing. Motsamai Mpho reacted by expelling Matante and Motsete from the party for failing to account for the missing funds. Thereupon Matante announced that he had also expelled Mpho.

Despite the fact that the BPP had split up into factions, its nationalist rhetoric had sufficiently alarmed the colonial administration and spurred it into looking for alternative nationalist leaders to lead Botswana to independence. Such was the suspicion about the BPP that the colonial administration even warned London that the party posed a serious threat to British interests in the colony, and that the only satisfactory opposition to the BPP would be a party headed by Seretse Khama (Gossett, 1986). The BDP was officially launched on 28 February 1962, as a counter weight to the BPP, which was seen by the colonial government as too radical because of its ties with the ANC (Motshidisi, 1975; Gossett, 1986). In fact the BDP was formed by some of the *Batswana* members of the Legislative Council. These were Seretse Khama, Quett Masire, Goareng S.Mosinyi, A.M.Tsoebebe, Tsheko T.Tsheko, J.Gugushe and A.Maribe. Others who were not in the Legislative Council but who played a crucial role in the formative years of the BDP were Moutlakgola Ngwako, Dabadaba Sedie, Amos Dambe and Benjamin Steinberg. According to Parsons (1995), Seretse Khama had used his position in the Legislative Council to establish his political image and that of the party that he later founded, the BDP, as the effective representative of the local intelligentsia and aspirant cattle owners. Because most of its leaders were in fact in the Legislative Council, between the time of its formation until the first general elections the BDP was in fact treated as the de facto government and was the incumbent party in the

37

1965 elections. Pickard (1985) argues that after its formation in 1962, the BDP received unqualified support from the colonial administration, and received financial and organisational support from the financially influential European and Asian communities which feared the more radical BPP coming to power. The party won the 1965 elections, and its leader, Seretse Khama, who was now one of the four members of the Executive Committee of the Legislative Council became the first Prime Minister and later the President of the Republic of Botswana. Gossett (1986, p. 8) argues:

> In effect, by commanding the support of the majority of the ... Legco [Legislative Council] members and having the sympathy of the [colonial] administration, the BDP became the ruling party without ever having fought an election or waged a nationalist struggle.

Admittedly, at the time of Independence, the petty bourgeois class that coalesced into the BDP was strong only at the political level. It was in control of the "new state" but had no firm economic base. It was therefore necessary that this petty bourgeoisie should transform the process of accumulation in such a way that it would generate a new centre of economic ownership and possession. With the formation of the BDP, the class of petty bourgeois nationalists broadened its social base to include some European commercial farmers and Asian traders. The absence of developed forces of production necessitated an alliance with international capital, a process that was perhaps initiated as far back as 1959 with the signing of copper mining agreement with the Rhodesian Selection Trust, and given an impetus by the arrival of De Beers in the country in 1967.

Development strategy as a class project

Since 1966, the Botswana state has overtly pursued a strategy of capitalist development. This strategy should be seen as an expression and outcome of specific class interests, whose roots go back to precolonial days. The decolonisation process of Botswana and the colonial administration's support for the BDP indicate that the political independence for Botswana was a result of a strategic compromise of the colonial power to transfer power to the local petty bourgeoisie that would safeguard the interests of metropolitan capital. As Amilcar Cabral (cited in Harris, 1975, p. 22) has argued:

> The objective of the imperialist countries [in granting political independence] was to prevent the enlargement of the socialist camp, to liberate the reactionary forces in [these] countries, which were stifled by colonialism, and to enable these forces to ally themselves with the international bourgeoisie. The fundamental objective was to create a bourgeoisie where one did not exist, in order to specifically strengthen the imperialist and capitalist camp.

38

As some of the postcolonial state policy pronouncements have made clear, the infrastructural developments undertaken by the state since Independence were there in order to create favourable conditions for the private sector to invest. These policies have been couched in the ideology of "national development", underlining the argument that each new class is compelled, merely to carry its aims, to represent its narrow interests as the common interests of the whole nation (Marx and Engels, 1970). The National Development Plan 5 (NDP 5) points out in no uncertain terms:

> The government is committed to active interventionist economic and social policies ... The government's commitment to planning *is not intended to stifle private initiative, but to create favourable conditions in which the private sector can contribute to Botswana's development*. The government's role in the economy [is to provide] the basic infrastructure of the country ... [and to take] responsibility for educating the labour force that the economy requires ... The government also sets the legal, fiscal and monetary framework within which all sectors operate and is responsible for securing favourable international economic arrangements for domestic producers ... (p. 61, emphasis added).

But where do state policies come from, and how are they determined? Who makes up the private sector in Botswana? The answers to these questions will emerge in the various parts of this analysis. Suffice it to point out here that for the class forces that emerged politically victorious in the run up to Botswana's independence in 1966, that is, the class of petty bourgeois nationalists who are represented politically in the ruling BDP, the postcolonial economic policies and strategies were a class project for private capital accumulation. A development strategy cannot be neutral. A development strategy is at the same time a class strategy. It indicates the general orientation of a regime with respect to the accumulation function. A development strategy also indicates which class or class fractions will take the main responsibility for expanding the economy and hence benefit from the accumulation of capital (Sandbrook, 1982, pp. 81-2). At the same time, the accumulation process engenders class formation, and aids the emergence of a class or alliance of class fractions with the economic power to ensure that the state henceforth represents primarily their interests.

As Alavi (1972) has argued, one characteristic feature of the colonial state is that it did not rest on the support of any of the local classes, but instead subordinated all the indigenous classes. The political independence of Botswana that came in 1966 marked the political restoration of a previous ruling class that had been living under colonial domination. The nationalist demands for independence in the 1950s and 1960s represented above all a resurgence of this class (Mogalakwe, 1983). Having been denied the opportunity to accumulate during the colonial period, the petty bourgeoisie entered into a alliance with international capital to enhance its economic position. At Independence, it accepted a liberal bourgeois constitution which gave the citizens all the democratic rights and freedoms associated with bourgeois democracy. It can be argued that this was partly because of the influence of the British. But it was also due to the fact that the new men in power wanted to end what they considered a backward political system based on royalty. Having delineated the class character of the Botswana state, we turn now to the examination of the functions of this "new state".

The postcolonial economic growth strategy

At the time of Independence, Botswana's gross domestic product was the equivalent of £12m and the income per capita was the equivalent of £25. The exports totalled the equivalent of £6m. The bulk of the exports consisted of meat (carcases), which amounted to the equivalent of £3m a year; this was followed by the export of labour (deferred pay and remittances), hides and skins and canned meat. The import bill was the equivalent of £7m in food, clothes and textile, building materials, machines, equipment, chemicals and drugs. In a population of 650,000, only 14,000 were in formal sector employment. There were 32,000 *Batswana* migrant workers in South Africa.[3] In order to transform the economy of the country, the government enunciated four economic planning objectives around which future development plans would be based. These four objectives were (a) rapid economic growth, (b) economic independence, (c) sustained development, and (d) social justice.[4]

(a) Rapid economic growth

It was the objective of the postcolonial state to ensure that the growth of the productive base of the economy would exceed population growth in order to sustain an increase in the average standards of living. To this end the new state sought to encourage production with more direct intervention in selected areas of the economy.

(b) Economic independence

Botswana was a small landlocked country bordering a large and economically developed country, South Africa. The state therefore had to lessen its vulnerability and dependence by mobilisation of internal resources, diversification of the economy and emphasis on training and localisation. Externally Botswana had to diversify its communication routes, its trade and investment partners and its sources of aid. According to NDP 5:

> Economic independence therefore became, for economic as well as political reasons, a major objective and one that has to temper the quest for rapid economic growth (p. 58).

40

Table 3.1
Selected social and economic indicators

	1965	1975-1976	1980-1981
GDP (P million, 1985-86 prices)	284	887.7	1,511.1
GDP per capita (Pula, 1985-86 prices)	537	1,071.8	1,615.5
Mining GDP (P million, 1985-86 prices)	-	144.4	530.3
Non-mining GDP (P million, 1985-86 prices)	-	743.3	980.8
Government GDP (P million, 1985-86 prices)	-	135.2	199.8
Formal employment (thousand)	14	57.3	83.4
Education			
Primary enrolment (thousand)	72	116.3	171.9
Secondary enrolment (thousand)	2	12.1	18.3
University enrolment	22	465	928
Primary school net enrolment rate (per cent)	-	72	92
Health			
Doctors per 100,000	5	-	15
Nurses per 100,000	6	-	124
Total hospital beds	-	-	2,060
Daily calorie supply per capita (number)	-	2,137	2,111
Access to safe water (per cent of population)	-	45	-
Kilometres of tarred roads	20	219	1,121
Number of registered privately owned motor vehicles (thousand)	4.5	15.4	27.3
Domestic electricity generation (million Kwh)	5	270	270
Telephone subscribers connected	-	-	-

Source: Ministry of Finance and Development Planning (1996), *Macro Economic Outline for National Development Plan 8.*

Table 3.1
(continued)

1985-1986	1990-1991	Most recent estimate	Date	Average annual growth rate
2,420.6	4,252.4	4,847.5	94/95	9.3
2,194.6	3,226.4	3,205.8	94/95	5.9
1,133.9	1,547.6	1,555.4	94/95	13.3
1,286.7	2,704.8	3,292.1	94/95	8.1
325.7	655.8	836.0	94/95	10.1
116.8	209.0	234.5	93/94	7.7
223.6	283.5	319.1	1995	5.2
32.2	56.9	104.7	1995	11.4
1,773	3,677	5,501	1995	13.1
93	91	89	1993	-
17	18	24	1994	3.4
156	216	217	1994	4.1
1,554	3,211	3,245	1994	3.2
2,310	2,392	2,468	1994	0.8
54	90	-	-	-
1,885	2,565	4,177	1994	16.8
45.7	74.4	101.5	1994	10.4
457	906	1,040	1995	7.0
10,079	22,195	43,487	1994	17.6

(c) Sustained development

The pattern of development was to be sustained by reinvesting resources generated from nonrenewable sources in order to enhance the economy's long term potential, and to exploit agricultural resources in such a way that they would not be destroyed.

(d) Social justice

Economic growth was not to be an end in itself but a means to other ends. A more productive economy was needed as the basis for the improved standards of living for *Batswana*, especially through employment.

Economic growth and structural transformations

According to Colclough and McCarthy (1980), the government's revenue from domestic sources increased from P4.5m to P28.1m in 1972-73. This was the first time that the recurrent budget was balanced after Independence. Over the same period, public development expenditure increased sixfold, from P5m to almost P30m, of which more than ten per cent was financed from domestic resources. By 1972-73 domestic production had almost quadrupled, allowing income per capita to triple over the same period. According to Colclough and McCarthy, the rate of economic growth was about 15 per cent per year between 1966 and 1973. The years from Independence up to 1996 saw very rapid economic growth and structural transformations in the country's social and economic landscape. These changes are captured in Table 3.1.

Table 3.1 gives indicators of physical, economic and social transformations since Independence. It takes 1965, the year in which Botswana was given self government, as the base line. The striking features of the table are the very high levels of growth in most areas of the economy. GDP per capita had increased from P537 in 1965 (in 1985-86 prices) to P3,200 in 1990-91. The most recent estimates at current prices put it at about P8,000. From 1965 to 1995 formal sector employment had increased from about 14,000 to about 234,500, and employment abroad (mainly in South Africa) fell from 31,000 in 1965 to about 12,000 in 1995. This represents a drop of about 61 per cent. Other notable infrastructural developments include building of a network of tarmacked roads, significant improvement in the transportation and communications network including a national microwave telephone network and an earth satellite link with most parts of the world. Education and primary health care are sectors where there have also been major improvements.

According to Table 3.2 , the biggest economic growth was in the mining sector, whose contribution to the total output increased from zero at the time of Independence to 51 per cent in 1988-89, or more than half of the GDP. However, by 1994-95 mining's contribution had declined to about 33 per cent of the GDP. Agricultural production declined from 39 per cent of the GDP in 1965 to 12.6 per cent in 1981 and fell to 4.2 in 1994. This means more people are now looking to the formal sector for employment. Other sectors also grew significantly in real terms. The public sector followed mining at 17.2 per cent of the GDP, followed by the commercial sector at 16.7 per cent. In terms of employment, the public sector has been the largest single employer.

Table 3.2
Gross domestic product by type of economic activity
(percentage of total)

	1981-1982	1984-1985	1986-1987	1988-1989	1990-1991	1992-1993	1994-1995
Agriculture	12.6	7.4	5.1	4.7	4.5	4.9	4.2
Mining	22.4	33.5	43.8	50.9	40.3	33.3	32.6
Manufacturing	7.8	5.8	6.0	5.0	4.8	4.9	4.7
Water and electricity	2.4	2.3	2.6	2.0	2.0	2.3	2.2
Construction	5.9	6.8	4.7	6.2	7.4	6.7	6.0
Trade, hotels and restaurants	20.2	17.6	13.7	10.5	14.2	15.8	16.7
Transport	2.8	3.0	2.1	2.4	2.8	3.5	3.5
Banks, insurance and business service	7.0	6.3	6.0	6.9	7.5	9.4	11.2
General government	17.4	16.1	15.2	10.2	14.9	17.2	17.2
Social and personal services	3.6	3.1	2.9	3.5	3.8	4.5	4.4
Dummy sector	(2.1)	(2.1)	(2.0)	(2.2)	(2.1)	(2.4)	(2.7)

Source: Ministry of Finance and Development Planning (1996), *Annual Economic Report*.

The state institutions of intervention

The economic growth and structural transformations just described can be attributed to two factors: (a) the discovery and profitable exploitation of diamond mining which increased government revenues and enabled the state to intervene indirectly through infrastructural developments, and (b) direct state intervention in the economy through the establishment of public companies. The Botswana state is committed to capitalism, and has been pursuing an overtly capitalist oriented strategy, including involvement in a joint venture with the giant South African multinational, De Beers. Botswana has acquired a 50 per cent equity in the diamond mining company, Debswana, with De Beers being the other partner. At the end of 1990, diamond mining contributed 60 per cent of government revenue (Jeffries, 1991).

Besides direct involvement in mining through Debswana, another area of significant state intervention was through the establishment of a number of public or state owned corporations (parastatals). The main ones are: the Botswana Meat Commission - BMC (formed in the mid 1950s), the Water Utilities Corporation (1970), the Botswana Power Corporation (1970), the Botswana Development Corporation - BDC (1970), the Botswana Housing Corporation (1971), the Botswana Livestock Development Corporation (1972), the Botswana Agricultural Marketing Board (1974) and the Botswana Telecommunications Corporation (1980). Other parastatals are the Bank of Botswana and Air Botswana. These state enterprises were created to fill the gap in the private sector provision, and their origin is related to the postcolonial economic development initiatives of providing the much needed infrastructure for the economy (Jeffries, 1991).[5] But as already pointed out above, Botswana's development strategy is at the same time a class project. Recently the government has made a policy decision to privatise some of these state corporations. According to the latest reappraisal of the public sector, government will "hive off" to the private sector some of the services provided by the public sector and thereby create more room within the domestic economy for the private sector to grow.[6]

There is a need to say something about the BDC because of the role that it plays in creating a "national bourgeoisie". The BDC is the country's primary development finance institution, with major shareholdings in joint ventures with a variety of firms across the economy (Harvey and Lewis, 1990; Jeffries, 1991). The BDC started operations in 1971. The objectives of the BDC are as follows: (a) infusion of share capital, short and long term loans and loan and overdraft guarantees, (b) procurement of industrial land and buildings, technical and managerial support, (c) promotion and development of new projects in the national interest, and (d) provision of expert business advice and guidance. The state owns all ordinary shares and BDC's international partners - NFM (Holland), the International Finance Corporation (World Bank), the Commonwealth Development Corporation (British) and D.E.G. (Germany) own preferential shares.[7]

The BDC's primary function is to identify and participate in the direction and control of viable enterprises. It is not just a passive loan giver or a sleeping partner. The BDC is an active participant in joint ventures with international capital, and supplies equity, loans, or debentures as and when it judges necessary or desirable on purely commercial calculations. Since its inception, the BDC has acted as a partner to both local and international capital in most industrial and commercial activities, and has acted mainly in a commercial and profit seeking way. By 1983 the BDC consisted of 27 subsidiaries, which in turn owned a further 15 subsidiaries. In addition, BDC held shares in 11 associated companies and financed four others directly by way of long term loans (Harvey and Lewis, 1990).

In 1989, the BDC Group underwent an organisational restructuring. The BDC Group now consists of two very huge departments: the projects department and the operations department. The projects department is responsible for developing new projects and serves as the first point of contact between a project sponsor and the Corporation. It evaluates investment proposals, negotiates investment terms and supervises the implementation of projects and the disbursement of loan and equity funds granted by the BDC. In the early 1990s, the projects department was involved in 25 projects, ranging from crocodile farming and the production of semiface clay bricks, to international hotels and a private hospital in Gaborone. The operations department is also active in various sectors of the country's economy, and is responsible for the monitoring and development of the investments. The operations department is organised in six divisions, all corresponding to the key sectors of the economy. These are: (a) industrial and commercial division, (b) agriculture, (c) transport, (d) hotels and tourism, (e) property management and development, and (f) financial services division.[8]

The Botswana state has been able to make these interventions in the economy largely because of the revenues that accrued to state coffers from diamond mining. Indeed the mining industry has had a positive knock on effect on the country's economy in the sense that the state has had enough revenues to develop the infrastructure. These in turn provided propitious conditions for private sector investment and development. To a large extent the overall objective of the postcolonial state of providing the necessary support for private sector development has been realised. This has led some analysts to argue that it was the discovery and profitable exploitation of diamond mining that was at the centre of Botswana's development and that diamond mining had become "the engine of growth" and "a launching pad" (Colclough and McCarthy, 1980; Harvey and Lewis, 1990; Stedman, 1993). Whilst there is much truth in this argument, the question that remains unanswered is this: since the diamond revenues were mostly invested in infrastructural development, where did the profit for private sector employers come from?

The manner in which the analysis of Botswana's political economy has been conducted leaves one with the impression that all is well as long as the necessary infrastructure is created and factories are built. For some analysts, the means of production are everything and the relations of production nothing. Because the key link for these analysts is not class struggle but the technical means of production, there is a lack of discussion of social relations and the working class appears as an aggregate number of employees. A detailed analysis of how labour actually contributed to the development of the country is undertaken in Chapter 4. Suffice it to point out here that to look only at mineral revenues alone in accounting for Botswana's postcolonial economic performance and to disregard the part played by labour is to give an inadequate and incomplete analysis of the political economy of a country.

The emergent national bourgeoisie

The term "national bourgeoisie" is used here to refer to the class or alliance of classes of national entrepreneurs who collectively pursue an economic strategy that increases the national share or control of the local economic processes. Depending upon particular conjunctures this class of national entrepreneurs may be in alliance with multinational capital or in competition with it (Kitching, 1987). My task in this section will be restricted to identifying the emergent national bourgeoisie in Botswana, by looking at areas of its participation in the local economy, that is, its main economic activities. Other characteristics of this class, such as its relative strength vis-à-vis foreign capital, its cohesiveness or lack of it, its political influence, if any, or whether it is a "comprador", "bureaucratic", "managerial" or whatever bourgeoisie, is a task that will be left to future research. Suffice is to point out again that colonialism had stifled the growth and development of indigenous entrepreneurial activities and the emergence of indigenous capital in Botswana is very much a postcolonial phenomenon. This is not to say that there was no propertied class in precolonial or colonial Botswana. Commercial ranching was, however, confined to Europeans farmers in the so called Crown Lands. These were fertile parts of the country that were designated by the colonial administration to resettle white farmers. But it was cattle farming that provided an impetus for capital accumulation even for indigenous *Batswana*.

Efforts to augment indigenous capital accumulation in the agricultural sector started in 1975 with the introduction of the Tribal Grazing Land Policy (TGLP). Under the TGLP the state gave incentives to large cattle owners to leave communal grazing areas and commercialise the livestock industry, which had hitherto been the domain of white *Batswana*. The TGLP was launched ostensibly for environmental reasons: to stop degradation of the land in communal areas. TGLP was viewed as a process of change from traditional and subsistence production of livestock towards a greater degree of market oriented production; a movement from a relatively lower level of production and low returns, to a relatively higher level of production and productivity and higher returns. The new commercial farmers were given incentives such as soft loans for fencing and borehole drilling and equipment. This assistance was, however, only for farmers with more than 200 cattle. The TGLP scheme was a class project which benefited only a small section of cattle

47

owners. This was the big traditional cattle owning class of petty bourgeois nationalists. These are the people who have, together with the white commercial farmers, dominated beef production and benefited from the guaranteed European market. For example, from 1979 to 1989, beef production from commercial farms accounted for about 42 per cent of sales at the Botswana Meat Commission. Under the Lome Convention, Botswana was entitled to export up to 19,000 tonnes of beef per annum to the European Economic Community (EEC) on preferential terms. Insofar as the domestic production of beef for world market was concerned, the national bourgeoisie has managed to exert significant control and derive large benefits. The average price per beast slaughtered at the BMC rose from P303 in 1985 to P653 in 1989, an increase of more than 100 per cent.

However, the TGLP was introduced against the background of the Rural Income Distribution Survey of 1974. Some of the findings of the survey were that only five per cent of the rural population own more than 50 per cent of the national cattle herd, and that 20 per cent of the population did not own any cattle at all. In 1980 fewer than 28 per cent of the rural households owned no cattle. This figure rose to 38 per cent in 1988. Rural households with less than 40 cattle declined from 51 per cent in 1980 to 48 per cent in 1988, and those with between 40 and 100 cattle declined from 14 per cent to 9 per cent in the same period (NDP 7).

Accumulation in other sectors of the economy has also proceeded apace, although it is not as impressive as in the commercial agricultural sector. In 1968, of the 439 shops registered in Botswana, only 31 per cent were *Batswana* owned (Best, 1970). By 1984, local ownership in the commercial sector had improved quite considerably. Of the 2,616 businesses in the commercial sector, 85 per cent were owned by *Batswana*, and only 15 per cent by foreigners (Selabe, 1988). However these were very small undertakings like bars and bottle stores (off licence), small general dealers (corner shops) and petrol stations. Jones-Dube (1992, p. 163) argues that having entered the already small commercial sector rather late, indigenous *Batswana* were operating under considerable disadvantages in terms of their late entry and due to constraints inherent in Botswana's economic position in southern Africa. As a result, *Batswana* businesses tended to lag behind those of Europeans and Asians in size, sophistication, profit making and expansion possibilities.

Ownership in the manufacturing sector gives important clues about the nature of capital accumulation. The progress made by *Batswana* petty bourgeoisie in this sector of the economy has not been very impressive, although by no means insignificant, considering where they were at the time of Independence. In 1982 the postcolonial state started a scheme called Financial Assistance Policy (FAP). The FAP has been described as a package of incentives for national and international investors to stimulate investment and create employment opportunities (NDP 7, p. 165). The FAP programme operates through a system of grants to provide financial support in the setting up or expanding private sector businesses in manufacturing and related activities, with emphasis on employment creation. Initially businesses could receive FAP support with fixed capital investment of up to P25,000 for a small scale project. The ceiling has since been raised to P75,000; medium scale project support has increased from P25,000 to P2m and large scale projects ceiling has now been raised from P900,000 to over P2m. Between 1985 and 1995, FAP financed about 5,314 businesses to the tune of about P722m. About 73 per cent of the projects financed under FAP in this period were small scale projects and accounted for only three per cent of the total investment. About 83 per cent of FAP funding, accounting for about 26 per cent of the projects, went to medium scale projects. Large scale projects accounted for only one per cent of the projects but for 14 per cent of the FAP funding (NDP 7, pp. 165-6). As it can be seen from these figures, the FAP is heavily weighted on the side of only a few large scale projects and like TGLP, it is another class project given a national character.

Table 3.3
Ownership of manufacturing firms
(selected years)

Year	Type of ownership				Citizen ownership as % of total
	Citizen	Joint	Foreign	Total	
1985	12	10	22	44	27
1990	165	120	190	475	35
1995	397	381	381	1,051	38

Source: Ministry of Commerce and Industry (1996).

The state's mission to create a "national bourgeoisie" has in a way met with some success. The most recent estimates put citizen ownership as percentage of total manufacturing at 38 per cent (Table 3.3). Although the participation of *Batswana* in the local economy has not grown by leaps and bounds as in countries where there has been an unambiguous "affirmative" action for indigenous capital (Kenya, for example) such participation has been growing steadily over the years. In order to promote such participation, the state passed the Trade and Liquor Act of 1986 to reserve for citizens certain businesses such as fresh produce, filling stations, bars and bottle stores. The hope is that participation in these businesses can be a launching pad for bigger things. It is now said that the state is concerned about the limited participation of *Batswana* in large undertakings like wholesale trade, chain stores, hotels and import and export, which continue to be dominated by noncitizens. Thus it will be the major challenge for the state in the 1990s to enable more *Batswana* to break into these relatively advanced business activities, which require greater financial and managerial capabilities (NDP 7, p. 162).

At the same time there has developed a "commercial bourgeois" class, which has benefited largely from land deals, property speculation, and inflated costs on state projects in the 1980s. Botswana, especially in the urban areas, is a land of contrasts: *bo-bashi* (street urchins) fight amongst themselves to wash imported German Mercedez Benz and BMW cars, or Japanese Toyota station wagons; palatial mansions on one side of the road and mud wall hovels on the other; old women scavenging the refuse dumps and five star restaurants are common sights in Gaborone. Conspicuous consumption and ostentation, the hallmark of the bourgeoisie in Western Europe and North America, has become the envy of the national bourgeoisie in the country (Parsons, 1993). Corruption and economic crimes have also taken root. The head of the Directorate of Corruption and Economic Crime recently pointed that the problems of corruption and economic crimes in Botswana are much more widespread and serious than the public are generally aware. Examples include official corruption, bribery and tax evasion involving millions of Pula.[9] Recently it was revealed that major cattle producers have been paying little or no income tax at all. The Income Tax Act allows cattle producers to price the cattle business below market rates for tax purposes, to declare losses on their cattle business and carry over these "losses" to other businesses. In 1992-93 cattle producers paid only P1.7m in taxes in an industry valued at P160m in beef exports to the European Community.[10] Meanwhile, the cabinet continues to veto recommendations on increasing tax on the livestock industry and extending labour rights to domestic workers, including farm workers (Mogalakwe, 1986).

The state and development: some observations

There is an ongoing debate as to whether countries at the periphery of capitalism can succeed in transforming their economies towards more modern industrial societies. This debate has focused on the degree of autonomy possible for indigenous accumulation under the external structural constraints imposed by the capitalist world economy and the state system (Lubeck, 1987). Some analysts like Taylor (1977) have argued that the economic penetration of the Third World by capitalism has resulted in an economic structure whose development is both highly uneven and necessarily restricted to particular sectors of the economy. Taylor further argues that in peripheral capitalism production for export is greater than production for domestic consumption and the domestic sector is characterised by low level technology which results in a low level of productivity; by contrast the export sector is characterised by high levels of productivity. The effects of these forms of penetration are that the possibilities for directing production towards the requirements of the indigenous economy are restricted. Yet others like Warren (1980), have argued that it should be possible to attain some economic development amidst these constraints. Warren gives examples of some countries from Asia and Latin America which in his view have succeeded or are on their way to some capitalist development. Kennedy (1988) puts the blame for lack of economic development in the African countries on the doorstep of the postcolonial state in Africa. He argues that postcolonial African governments have tended to act in ways that obstruct rather than encourage African capitalism because of the failure to provide assistance and to create a favourable national economic climate within the limitations set by the international situation. He argues that the state and politics have had a particularly profound and often retarding effect on indigenous economic activity of all kinds, including emergent capitalists and that the state's own economic activities have stifled enterprise investment.

In his criticism of Botswana's political economy, Parson (1980) starts by analysing what he identifies as the limits of capitalist transformation imposed on Botswana by South Africa. He argues that the limits to Botswana's ability to generate an autocentric process of development arise from its Constitution as a particular kind of dependent capitalist country, a significant component of which has been its geographical position on the periphery of South Africa, and that the development efforts of a developing country are subject to the vagaries of the world economy.

It will be fair to put Taylor (1977) in the category of world system theory and Parson (1980) in that of dependency theory. These schools of thought tend to place undue emphasis on a country's external linkages (external determination), especially if those linkages are of a dependent or unequal nature. The role of the state in redirecting the process of accumulation is given a secondary consideration. This is a pessimistic view which also has serious flaws for analysing a country such as Botswana. As we have seen, the state has made a significant advance in modernising the economy by transforming a backward agrarian economy into a fairly modern one within a space of 30 years.

On the basis of the empirical overview of the Botswana's political economy that I have given, I find the pessimistic scenario of Taylor and Parson difficult to accept. But at the same time Warren, who represents the more orthodox Marxist approach (internal determination), expresses a rather optimistic view which is also based on a limited number of countries. On the other hand, Kennedy stands on his own. Contrary to what he argues, in Botswana the transformation of the economy has been spearheaded by the state in alliance with both indigenous capital interests and international or multinational capital. Lacking in technical and managerial expertise, marketing channels and resource, the state and indigenous capital have deeply involved themselves with South Africa, the USA and Britain and with German capital. The beginning of the 1990s saw the arrival of more multinationals from South Korea, France, Kuwait, Lebanon and the People's Republic of China.

It may argued that the presence of international or multinational capital in Botswana serves to highlight the pessimism of the dependency theorists. But in the current phase of the internationalisation of capital, it may be naïve not to expect indigenous capital to engage in joint ventures with international capital. It is only through joint ventures that both the state and indigenous capital can acquire the technology and the organisational expertise to deepen the level of indigenous capital accumulation. Lubeck (1987, p. 12) argues that the seminal question should be how the group identified as the national bourgeoisie is involved in the national economy, and how its participation transforms the economy and alters the balance of class forces in the society.

Conclusion

The foregoing empirical analysis of the political economy of Botswana from Independence to about 1990 has revealed the class character of the postcolonial Botswana state and has delineated the functions of this state, especially with regard to social and physical infrastructural development. It has been argued that these are the traditional functions of the state. Every society has to reproduce the conditions of production at the same time as it produces and a society that does not do this will not last. In order to achieve this, the state in the capitalist society intervenes to provide the necessary conditions for economic growth and development. This process has resulted in class formation. During this process, some groups of people have been able to increase their wealth and power, whilst the wealth and power of others have declined. A large class of the urban proletariat has emerged alongside a small class of the petty bourgeoisie and the bourgeoisie. The petty bourgeoisie is the one involved in small businesses and the bourgeoisie is the one which has been able to break into the manufacturing sector and commercial agriculture. As pointed out, these two classes have benefited directly from the state policies such as the Trade and Liquor Act, FAP and TGLP. It is on this basis that it can be argued that state policies only appear neutral, whilst in practice they help some sections of the people at the expense of others, usually the majority.

The Botswana state has also been involved in infrastructural development and in the management of the economy through the BDC. Admittedly, in Botswana, as in most peripheral formations, the state's involvement in economic management tends to be much more direct and obvious. But even in developed capitalist countries, the state is also involved in economic management and development. Duncan (1989, p. 3) argues that in the 1980s, public sector spending in the Organisation for European Cooperation and Development countries accounted for 45 per cent of all economic activity, reaching up to 67 per cent in the case of the Netherlands. The involvement of the state in economic management and development is therefore a common phenomenon in both developed and developing countries. The emphasis on economic growth and economic independence helps the national bourgeoisie and enhances national sovereignty. The involvement of the state in economic management and development and in infrastructural development in Botswana is a long term strategy by the petty bourgeoisie which controls the postcolonial state, to create what it describes as "favourable conditions for private sector development". This means securing conditions for private capital accumulation.

This is what makes the Botswana state a capitalist state. The state is "capitalist" in the sense that it has structural links with the economically dominant classes, and because it is actually helping nurture private capital accumulation through schemes such as TGLP and FAP. The state is also capitalist, firstly because it is the largest single employer of labour; secondly, as a partner with international capital it is involved in the valorisation of capital. The form of the Botswana state as a capitalist state is, however, revealed in its relation to labour.

Notes

1. The traditional *Tswana* society comprised several *merafe* - communities (derogatorily called tribes by the British), each living in large villages within a given geographical space described as *kgaolo* or district. Each *morafe* was headed by a *kgosi* (also called a chief or a king), or a presidential monarch with executive powers. The social patterns and institutions of all *Batswana* are similar - regardless of the geographical space they occupy.

2. See the *Bechuanaland Protectorate Credit Sales to Natives Proclamation,* No. 38, promulgated on 3 August 1923.

3. *Transitional Plan for National Development* (1966), p. 3.

4. *National Development Plan 5*, pp. 2-5.

5. Most of the developed capitalist countries started their industrialisation about 150 years ago. Britain for instance started in the 1790s. Other countries like France started in the 1830s, USA - in the 1840s, Germany - in the 1850s, Japan - in the 1870s and Canada - in the 1890s. Amongst developing countries are Argentina (1935), Turkey (1937), China and India (1952).

6. Botswana's Vice President and Minister of Finance and Development Planning, in *The Botswana Daily News,* No. 105, 5 June 1996, p. 2.

7. Seretse Khama's address to the workers at Selebi Phikwe, 19 December 1975.

8. *Botswana Development Corporation Annual Reports*, 1988.

9. *Mmegi Wa Dikgang,* 16 September 1995; *The Gazette*, 29 March 1995.

10. *The Gazette,* 10 July 1996.

4 The capitalist form of the Botswana state

Introduction

Capitalism is predicated on the institutional separation of the polity from the economy in such a way that the state appears autonomous or removed from economic processes. These economic processes, however, depend upon specific modes of state intervention in the economy, such as infrastructural development and other conditions that the apparently autonomous state provides. The inability of capitalism to guarantee its economic self generation and the reliance of the state on the revenues from private capital imply a symbiotic relationship between the state and capital. It is this structural link between the state and capital that reveals the state as a capitalist state (Strinati, 1979).

This chapter examines some of the mechanisms used by the Botswana state to secure "favourable conditions" for capital accumulation in the postcolonial era. This included formulating a wages policy that made Botswana a low wage economy. The state also created the necessary state apparatuses for the monitoring and implementation of this policy. It is this low wages policy that reveals the Botswana state as a capitalist state. It is argued that though this low wages policy may have facilitated economic growth, it also led to very unequal income distribution and the maintenance of poverty wages for the majority of wage earners in Botswana.

The wages policy (1972-90)

As already indicated, at the time of Independence Botswana was an economically backward and poor country. Soon after Independence, the state embarked on a policy of industrialisation and rapid economic growth. The National Development Plan 1970-75 (NDP) stated the major economic goals for the country were to secure the fastest possible rate of economic growth and a rapid expansion of employment opportunities. In 1970, Professor Dharam Ghai was engaged to study

Botswana's economic position and to make necessary recommendations. The consultant's terms of reference were:

> To study the present structure and level of salaries, in Botswana, and to draft a long term wages policy, consonant with the National Development Plan. The wages policy should include criteria for establishing recommended wage structure, minimum wage levels and wage differentials. The expert must bear in mind Botswana's need to retain a competitive economic position in relation to its neighbours, and that labour costs are a critical aspect of this problem.[1]

Ghai noted that Botswana was a very poor country, even by standards of developing countries in Africa, which themselves were among the poorest in the world. Ghai pointed out that the 1968 figures show that the country had a per capita income of only R67, and that if the salaries of expatriates were discounted, the per capita income would come down to a mere R50. Since the economic objectives were already clearly set out in the NDP, the consultant advised that Botswana could take one of two options: either to have a small but relatively highly paid labour force in the modern formal sector, or a larger but lowly paid labour force. He argued that:

> ... socially higher wages will have the effect of reducing employment, at a given level of income, forcing employers to use the labour force more efficiently, leading to higher productivity per employee; lead to a reduction in the labour force due to mechanisation and other labour saving devices; stimulate migration from rural areas ... high costs of labour will lower profitability of investment, and lead to reduced investment through reduction in the inflow of foreign capital; retard the industrial development of the country and limit the expansion of exports where prices are determined in the world market.

The second choice was one that:

> ... will have the opposite effect to those of the high wage economy. It will lead to a less efficient use of labour, with lower productivity, higher volume of employment, lower unemployment, lower rural-urban income gap, reduced migration from rural areas, higher levels of investment, and a more rapid expansion of the quantity and quality of public services.[2]

Ghai further recommended that in order to stop wages in what he called "privileged highly capital intensive industries" to rise to excessively higher levels, the government should seek powers to approve all wage agreements. Most of Ghai's recommendation were accepted by the government and in 1972 were translated into a wages policy.[3]

The wages policy stated that because there were certain special skills that were vital to the economy, there should be no competition for skilled labour amongst various sectors of the economy. In other words, salaries and wages should not follow the law of supply and demand. It was felt that high wages offered by one sector of the economy or by a particular employer would affect the allocation of skilled labour by attracting workers to that sector or employer, thereby creating shortages in other sectors or enterprises. This situation was found to be undesirable.[4] The state took steps to ensure that the public and private sectors do not enter into what was regarded as "unprofitable competition for scarce resources". The policy emphasised that there should not be any competition in the various sectors of the economy for the inadequate pool of trained workers as this would force up wages and salary levels without necessarily improving labour productivity.[5]

To this end, the government moved on to fix minimum wages for the unskilled labour force and maximum levels for the skilled labour force. According to the wages policy, minimum wages in the urban areas would be equal to the average rural income of farmers, with an allowance for any differential in the overall costs of urban living. Insofar as salaries and wages for skilled labour were concerned, the policy stated that:

> Basic local wages and salary levels in the private and parastatal sectors should generally conform to, and on no account significantly exceed those paid by government to comparable grades of public employees ... Government will review wages and salaries in the public sector on a regular basis, and the private sector and the parastatals should not anticipate the outcome of such reviews by granting premature increases.[6]

Though the wage and salary reviews were supposed to take into consideration such factors as economic conditions prevailing at the particular time, a proven increase in the cost of living and an increase in labour productivity, the wages policy emphasised that there could be no guarantee that wages and salaries would be increased in step with inflation. This "formula" remained the point of reference in all matters of wage and salary determination from 1972 to 1990, and marks a period I characterise as the second phase of Botswana's peripheral capitalist development. From the time of the inception of the wages policy in 1972 until 1990 the state was the wage leader, and public officers' wages and salaries were used as bench marks to determine the wage and salary structure in the private and parastatals organisations. The state was also the largest single employer. The share of the state in total employment at the time of the inception of the wages policy was 33 per cent. After increasing in the mid 1970s, the state's share fell back to 33 per cent in 1981. At the time of economic liberalisation in 1990, the state's share of total employment (including parastatals) was 36.5 per cent. In 1995, the state share was about 42 per cent (Mogalakwe et al., 1996).

The question of the cost of public sector employment in most developing countries has always been a very thorny issue. The state develops a direct interest in regulating industrial relations and its predominance in the economy leads to the process of collective bargaining becoming "trilateral" instead of "bilateral" in that wage determination is not a matter for trade unions and management alone. The intention of the petty bourgeoisie which controls the state is to keep the cost of the public sector employment deliberately low so as to pay for infrastructural development.

In many developing countries this has become one way of influencing wage trends: the state exerts indirect pressure on the general wage level because of the preponderance of the public sector employment, and most undertakings model their wage structure on the public sector wage and salary structure. Thus the decisions taken by the state have a substantial effect on the level of remuneration in the private sector. Its example becomes the standard bearer for the regulation of employment in other sectors (Sandbrook and Cohen, 1975; Caire, 1977; Bean, 1985).

Framework for implementation

The 1972 White Paper advised that if the proposed wages policy was to be enforced according to government's wishes and intentions, there was a vital necessity to monitor its implementation and to establish machinery to coordinate and elaborate the policy in all its details.[7] To this end a tripartite structure, the National Employment, Manpower and Incomes Council (NEMIC), was created. NEMIC comprised seven permanent secretaries, four members from the private sector, two members from the trade union movement and one member from the public sector employees.

Since its creation in 1972, NEMIC has been under the chairmanship of the Assistant Minister of the Ministry of Finance and Development Planning (MFDP).[8] Its terms of reference included reviewing the overall trends in incomes, prices and profits in the light of the national policy and making recommendations as appropriate. NEMIC would made recommendations to the government on proposed salaries and wages in the public sector. Government would then announce its award to the public sector employees. The private sector would then adopt the same percentage increase with little or no consultation with the trade unions (Frimpong and Olsen, 1985).

Since NEMIC's terms of reference did not contain mechanisms of determining wages and salaries in the private sector, another structure, the Wages Policy Committee (WPC) was created to process and approve private and parastatal sector wages and salaries. Like NEMIC, it was also chaired by the Assistant Minister of MFDP and its secretary was a senior economist in the employment policy unit at the MFDP. But unlike NEMIC, the members of the WPC were all senior state officials and there was no representative from the private sector employers or from the trade unions. The membership consisted of the following:

1 The Secretary for Economic Affairs, MFDP.

2 The Administrative Secretary, Office of the President.

3 The Deputy Director, Directorate of Public Service Management (DPSM).

4 The Deputy Permanent Secretary, Ministry of Land and Home Affairs (MLHA).

5 The Commissioner of Labour.

6 A job analyst, DPSM.

The terms of reference of the WPC were: (a) to review proposals for increases in wage rates in the private and parastatals sector, and to determine the extent to which these may be justified in the light of the incomes and localisation policies, (b) to advise employers of any modifications or additions to these proposals that may be necessary, and (c) to advise the minister concerned on the need to establish wage councils in any particular sector and to review existing wages regulation orders. According to Colclough and Olsen (1985) the WPC was established as a "watch dog" committee to monitor the implementation of the wages policy and ensure that the private sector wages and salaries did not significantly exceed those being paid in the public sector. In July 1974, following the Wage Regulation Orders promulgation, five wage councils were established to supplement the WPC. The five wage councils were for:

1 Building and construction.

2 Hotels and catering.

3 Garage and motor trade.

4 Wholesale, retail and distributive trades.

5 Manufacturing trades.

These councils, which were in effect WPC subcommittees, met regularly to determine minimum rates and hours of work for each of the five sectors. In addition, the councils laid down regulations for annual leave, overtime rates and public holidays. The councils were consolidated by the 1982 Employment Act which established a single Minimum Wages Advisory Board in the place of the five wage councils (Colclough and Olsen, 1985).

It would seem that the WPC was effective in its "mission" to cut wages and salaries. Between 1974 and 1980 it reviewed the wages and salaries of some 30 private and parastatal organisations including major mining houses, commercial banks and a number of the large manufacturing, retail and hotel organisations, accounting for about 40 per cent of nongovernmental formal sector employment. It succeeded in bringing basic wages and salaries in line with those of government and in accordance with the wages policy. In one case, the WPC reduced a company's wage bill by about P78,000 a month (Colclough and Olsen, 1985).

The cornerstone of the wages policy, and one which the WPC adhered to very strictly, was the so called job to job comparison, in which the government insisted that comparability must be maintained between a job in the public sector and a "similar" job in the private sector. The job to job comparison seldom took into account factors such as technical complexity, productivity, the specialised nature of the job or its level of responsibility (Presidential Commission, 1990). Although wages and salaries in some sectors like mining, railways, meat processing and banking were renegotiated biennially, such agreements had to be vetted by the WPC (Frimpong and Olsen, 1985).

In its attempt to augment capital accumulation, the state tended to be enthusiastic and protective towards the private sector. For example in 1978, under pressure from the WPC, the commercial banks management had to withdraw a salary deal with the banks' supervisory and middle managerial staff (Frimpong and Olsen, 1985). In 1983 the state rejected recommendations for a review of the wages policy in which the consultants had recommended that the government should abandon the job to job comparison and allow the private sector to determine salary grading and structure for specific groups within approved salary bands. The recommendations were rejected on the grounds that their implementation would vitiate the wages policy.[9]

The enthusiasm to protect and nurture private capital accumulation was, however, not always in the best interests of individual accumulators because the policy was applied strictly, without reference to a firm's profitability or ability to pay and compete. The constraints of the policy were highlighted in an interview with the personnel manager of one wholesale company. According to the personnel manager, his company, Sefalana Sa Botswana, had advertised for the position of a driver for one of their articulated lorries. The advertisement stated the salary to be offered. According to the manager, among the letters that they received responding to the advertisement was one from the Secretary of the WPC (MFDP), objecting to the salary offer on the basis that it contravened the wages policy. According to the manager, what was surprising to them as management was that the government had objected without knowing what the job actually entailed. As the manager pointed out:

The government objected to a driver being given P900 per month, just because he was a driver. But this driver was going to be driving a truck worth hundreds of thousands of Pula, and crossing the border carrying goods from South Africa worth millions of Pula. The company was prepared to pay the driver that amount because we did not want him to disappear with our merchandise.[10]

This incident shows the extent to which the state was prepared to go to safeguard the interests of capital as a whole, even in cases in which such intervention was not in the best interests of a particular capitalist. The significance of the WPC as a state apparatus charged with the responsibility of monitoring the wages policy was not only in the fact that it was staffed exclusively by senior state officials but that it excluded the people whose interests it was supposed to serve - the private sector employers, thus keeping the competing interests of individual capital away from the state arena.

Salary review commissions

In addition to the institutional structures that were set up to monitor the observance of the wages policy, the government regularly reviewed wages and salaries of public sector employees, in keeping with the spirit of the 1972 wages policy. The government reviewed public sector wages and salaries on a regular basis, taking into consideration economic conditions of that time and any proven increase in the cost of living. From the time of the inception of the wages policy until the early 1990s, wages and salaries of public sector employees were reviewed through a series of salary review commissions. The first of such reviews was done in 1974 by the Makgekgenene Salaries Commission. It was followed by the Chiepe Salaries Commission in 1976, the Mmusi Salaries Commission in 1978, the Meswele Salaries Commission in 1980 and the Gasennelwe Salaries Commission in 1982. The last was the Temane Salaries Commission in 1992. All these commissions except the 1982 one were chaired by cabinet ministers. Like the NEMIC and the WPC, the commissions were also dominated by top civil servants, or managers of private sector and parastatals organisations, again with only a token representation from the labour movement. Since 1992 the system of appointing salaries review commissions was replaced with an annual inflation adjustment across the board.

In 1989 the government appointed a Presidential Commission to review the 1972 wages policy. The commission presented its findings in 1990. One of its major recommendations was that the 1972 wages policy should be abandoned and that the government must deregulate the labour market. The commission pointed out that the wages policy had restricted labour mobility and killed incentives, and impeded the growth of collective bargaining. The commission advised that greater flexibility in the setting up of wages was a necessary condition for expanding the quantity, quality and efficient use of labour.[11] This marked the beginning of a neoliberal

Table 4.1
Estimated earnings by economic activity and citizenship of employees
(March 1991)

Economic Activity	Citizen employees	Average monthly earning (Pula)	Noncitizen employees	Average monthly earning (Pula)
Agriculture	6,499	216	177	3,575
Mining and quarrying	7,447	733	359	5,850
Manufacturing	24,803	456	1,220	3,478
Electricity and water	2,397	984	115	5,317
Construction	31,272	424	2,558	2,119
Commerce	39,757	378	1,288	2,398
Transport and communication	8,698	761	392	2,216
Finance and business services	14,352	821	1,792	3,457
Community and personal services	7,931	473	675	1,303
Education	1,925	869	615	3,562
Subtotals				
Private	*133,828*	*462*	*8,673*	*5,108*
Parastatals	*11,253*	*926*	*521*	*2,642*
Central government	62,466	737	12,079	2,677
Local government	12,866	596	108	2,170
Total all sectors	*211,413*	*66*	*11,381*	*2,762*

Source: Central Statistics Office (1992), *Labour Statistics*.

phase in Botswana's peripheral capitalist development. The analysis of the implications of this phase for the labour movement is undertaken in the final chapter. For the moment I would like to turn to a discussion on the effects and impact of these economic growth and wage policies on income distribution and social inequality.

Income distribution and social inequality

It is characteristic of bourgeois economists to measure the economic performance of a country only in terms of gross domestic product and per capita income levels. Countries with higher levels of GDP or per capita income are seen as performing well economically.

It is important, however, to realise that neither of these measurements adequately addresses questions of distribution or social equality (Thirlwall, 1989; Nafziger, 1988). For example, the GDP is a measure of the total output of goods and services which encompasses income earned within a country's boundaries. What can be misleading for a Third World country like Botswana is that such a measure includes income earned by foreign residents and companies, even if this income is transferred abroad. At the same time, per capita income is a measure of the average social wealth and does not address the problem of distribution. It is therefore important that these measures are used with caution, especially because they can increase side by side with growing social inequalities.

In other words, social inequalities and poverty are not incompatible with high levels of economic growth. Whilst higher levels of GDP and per capita income may make a country look respectable on paper, this does not necessarily mean the position of its citizens is any better. For instance, as Table 4.1 illustrates, although in all sectors of the Botswana economy people with the highest salaries are expatriates, the calculation of both the GDP and per capita income does not take this into account. Consequently those not familiar with the political economy of Botswana may expect the higher levels of GDP and per capita income to reflect higher levels of incomes. But as the table shows, the average monthly earnings of a *Batswana* worker was a paltry P566 per month compared to the average earnings of an expatriate at P2,762 a month.

Though one of the guiding principles of the 1972 wages policy was to achieve social justice and equitable distribution of the country's income and wealth, in practice this proved to be nothing but a platitude. What seems to be the case is that income inequality in Botswana has increased as the country has become richer. In Botswana, as in most peripheral capitalist economies, the problem of distribution emanates from the pattern of economic growth, rather than from the rate of growth. Though the levels of per capita income have actually increased substantially since Independence in most Third World countries, the available evidence suggests that the growth that has taken place has served largely to benefit the richest 20 per cent of the population. Usually income inequality is considered high if the income share of the bottom 40 per cent of the population is less than 12 per cent of the GDP (Sandbrook, 1982; Thirlwall, 1989).

The first income distribution survey in independent Botswana was in 1974, when the Central Statistics Office (CSO) carried out a Rural Income Distribution Survey (commonly known as RIDS), the results of which have been extensively used in the debate about Botswana's income distribution. According to RIDS, in 1974, about ten years after Independence, the poorest 40 per cent of the rural households had less than 12 per cent of the national income whilst the richest 20 per cent of the rural households had 58 per cent of the national income. The Gini coefficient - the measure of relative inequality, was 0.52. Whilst this could be explained away as a colonial legacy that had left the country economically stagnant for 80 years, income inequality has steadily increased.

In 1985-86 and again in 1993-94, the CSO conducted a comprehensive Household Income and Expenditure Survey (HIES) which covered both rural and urban areas. According to the 1985-86 HIES, the overall distribution of income (that is, cash and income in kind) was such that the poorest 40 per cent of the population earned only 10.7 per cent of the total national income, the next 40 per cent earned 27.8 per cent of the national income, and the richest 20 per cent of the population earned 61.5 per cent of the total income. The Gini coefficient in 1986 was 0.56, up by four points from the 1974 level. The HIES revealed further that 12 per cent of the national income went to only one per cent of the population, and that 35 per cent of the national income goes to only five per cent of the population and further that the lower ten per cent of the population has only three per cent of the national income. The survey further revealed that 73.9 per cent of urban households had an income of less than P500 per month, while on the other hand a mere 4.4 per cent of the urban households had income of P2,000 or above a month. This income inequality was greater in the rural households, where only 0.3 per cent of the households earned P2,000 or more a month. Altogether, only 1.4 per cent of all the households in the country earned more than P2,000 per month.

The 1993-94 survey showed only a marginal decrease in the gap between the rich and the poor in Botswana. In fact compared to 1974 the gap has actually widened, despite impressive growth in the economy, as measured by per capita income. The income share of the poorest 40 per cent in 1993-94 was 11.6 per cent, up by less than one percentage point from 1985. The next 40 per cent earned 20.1 per cent and the richest 20 per cent earned 59.3 per cent. The Gini coefficient was 0.537 compared to 0.556 in 1985-86. The 1993-94 HIES revealed that the extent of income inequality was worse in urban areas, where income inequality was at 0.539. This worsened to 0.638 if disposable cash income only was used in the calculation. Figure 4.1 summarises the pattern of income distribution from 1976 to 1993-94.

This pattern of income distribution is quite consistent with the assumption often made that workers do not deserve higher salaries because of their natural propensity to consume (Sandbrook, 1982). According to this economic logic, it is in the interests of the nation (meaning employers, traders and property owners) that more income should accrue to people who can save and invest. The rhetoric justifying this in Botswana, as in most developing countries, has been the need to create employment and promote national development. And this has been reinforced by the argument that higher wages and salaries will drive away investors because Botswana will become a high wage economy. The trade union movement has tried unsuccessfully to fight against this position, arguing that there is no evidence to support the argument that low wages create jobs for the unemployed or deprive the peasantry of income, and that profit is only a potential source of investment, not an automatic source. This fact is of course illustrated by the conspicuous consumption of the business community in Botswana.[12]

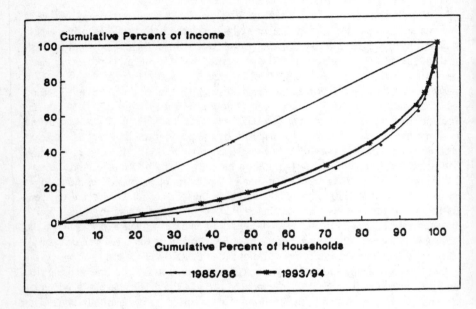

Figure 4.1 Lorenz curves for 1985-86 and 1993-94
Source: Central Statistics Office, *HIES (1985-86) and HIES (1993-94)*.

The heart of the matter is that there is no evidence that high wages will have a negative effect on economic development by reducing the volume of employment or slowing its growth as unskilled labour becomes more expensive and employers seek to economise in its use by substituting machines for labour, while some firms find it impossible to pay the higher wage rates and are forced out of business (Caire, 1977).

The Presidential Commission noted the problem of high inequality in income distribution in Botswana but reacted in a way that sought to explain away the problem by just blandly stating that comparative household income distribution shows that Botswana is not dissimilar in that with other African countries for which data are present, and that income in these countries is fairly inequitably distributed.[13] Though the commission did not indicate where it stood in connection with this issue, it is worth noting that conventional development economic wisdom always takes it as a given fact that it is natural and consistent with laws of development economics that there should be a highly unequal distribution of income in developing countries (Kuznets, 1955).

According to this conventional wisdom, owing to the dual character of the developing countries economies, inequality follows an inverted U shaped curve, first increasing, and eventually decreasing with economic growth. This is supposed to have happened to the now developed capitalist countries of Europe and North America in their earlier phases of development. This conventional wisdom suggests that productivity and therefore incomes are higher in the modern sector than in the traditional sector, and that as the modern sector expands, more and more people will be absorbed into it and start getting better income as a result of their participation in the modern sector. Thus gradually the inverted U shaped curve of income distribution skews to the right, and income distribution will become less unequal, very much like in the developed capitalist countries, where inequality of income distribution is relatively low. According to Nafziger (1990, pp. 102-115), however, even in the developed capitalist countries, the income share of the bottom 40 per cent of the population is less than 20 per cent of the gross national product. There is no guarantee therefore that as the country develops, inequality in income distribution will lessen. Argentina and Brazil are examples of countries where inequality in income distribution has not come down despite economic growth, while in Sri Lanka income inequality has declined despite low income levels. The inverted U shaped pattern of income distribution, even if assumed historically correct, is not inevitable, but a consequence of economic growth policies that place the highest priority on growth, while incorrectly assuming that profits will trickle down to the poor.

Conclusion

The organising principle of capitalism is the relationship between wage labour and capital within a system of generalised commodity production and exchange in which the materials and equipment are combined with labour to produce outputs (goods or services) which are sold by their owners for a profit. To realise profit, the owner of the means of production must exploit labour, that is to say, reward labour below its value. Exploitation of labour is defined as the ratio of unpaid labour to paid labour. In the foregoing analysis, it has been revealed that the Botswana state, through the low wages policy and the state apparatuses that it created to monitor the implementation of this wages policy, was sustaining the process of private capital accumulation. The Botswana state is therefore not a neutral state. It is situated in capitalism and sustains its logic by maintaining a specific pattern of relations of production. The state is therefore implicated in the generation and distribution of surplus value. The Botswana state's structural links with the capitalist economy serve to secure the conditions of existence of capitalism not only through the maintenance of this pattern of ownership, but also through the ideological manipulation and political domination of the working class, as I will show in the next chapter.

Notes

1   See Professor Ghai's covering letter on his report, *A Long Term Wages Policy For Botswana*, 28 May 1970. It is well worth noting that in this report, Ghai talked about a wages policy, and the need for wages restraint, and not about an incomes policy. I will therefore use the term "wages policy" rather than the preferred "incomes policy". This is so because though this policy was supposed to regulate prices, profit and rent, that did not happen. The policy was more directed to wages and salaries.

2   Op. cit., pp. 7-8.

3   *Republic of Botswana Government White Paper*, No. 2 on National Policy on Incomes, Employment, Prices and Profits, 1972.

4   Op. cit., pp. 4-5.

5   Ibid.

6   Ibid.

7   Ibid.

8   The representation is token because trade union representatives are usually vastly outnumbered by state functionaries and private sector representatives; in effect trade unions' representation is just symbolic and merely makes them just junior partners in the whole process. Trade union officials have been involved in most of the salaries review commissions.

9   Presidential Commission, p. 49.

10   Interview with Mr Mookodi, personnel manager at Sefalana, 6 February 1992.

11   Presidential Commission, pp. 66-69.

12   Botswana Federation of Trade Unions Policy Proposal on the Regulation of Wages and Salaries, Prices, Profits and Rents (not dated).

13   Presidential Commission, p. 28.

5 The state and the trade unions

Introduction

Capitalism is not just about the production of things; it is simultaneously about the production of social relations and ideas about those relations (Braverman, 1974; Althusser, 1971). To understand this process, one should look at growth in employment not only in quantitative terms where workers are discussed as an inert category or aggregate number of employees in a factory, but as a part of a dynamic social process that entails definite social relations of production. This chapter examines the perceptions and attitudes of the postcolonial petty bourgeois state elite about the role of the trade unions in development. This perception of and attitude to the role of trade unions in development should be placed against the class character and form of the Botswana state as a capitalist state. It is argued that in order to alleviate the class contradictions that have been engendered by the postcolonial economic growth policies, the petty bourgeois state elite responded with an attempt to inculcate in the minds of the workers a labour discipline that would remove or at least minimise the threat posed by the working class to the process of capital accumulation.

I start by discussing the strategies of the postcolonial state to restructure and remodel the trade union movement, the formation of the Botswana Federation of Trade Unions (BFTU), the role played by some international labour organisations in inculcating capitalist labour discipline, and the exhortations of the petty bourgeois state elite to the trade union movement to accept sacrifice in the interests of "national development". I shall also refer to speeches and policy statements by the first President of Botswana, Seretse Khama, and some of his colleagues, on the role of the trade unions in development. These speeches emphasise what I identify as the four principles of industrial relations in Botswana: wages restraint, industrial peace, political stability and national development. These principles give vital clues to the postcolonial state trade union philosophy and the model of trade unions that we have in Botswana. This model can be characterised as a "corporate nationalist" model, with its stress on the commonality of interests between state, capital and labour. Political activism by the trade union movement is discouraged and strike actions though legal, are virtually impossible (Kraus, 1979).

From the very beginning the state adopted a paternalistic attitude in the name of "national interest", "industrial peace" and "social justice" by providing the so called floor of rights and minimum legislation to protect workers. These points will be elaborated in the chapters that follow. Suffice here to point out that the measures taken by the state against the trade unions were motivated by the desire on the part of the state elite to neutralise trade unions as possible centres of opposition to the new economic and social policies envisaged by this elite (Gladstone, 1980). These forms of control used by the state and employers are often referred to in the current literature on labour studies as "habituation". Habituation is a process embarked upon to make the working class acquiescent or supportive of the exploitative social relations of production. It refers to the process of forming a "new habit" in the worker, that is, adjusting the worker to the labour process in its capitalist form, in order to overcome resistance (Braverman, 1974; Crisp, 1984; Cohen and Henderson, 1991).

The state, as the guarantor of private capital accumulation, seeks to control labour and to maximise surplus value extraction through the control of wages. This proceeds through making or persuading the workers to accept the system of unequal distribution of the product of their labour and unequal distribution of effort and authority in the labour process (Crisp, 1984, pp. 1-7). Habituation also includes "interior determination", a process which involves the transmission of elements of culture and ideology which become accepted or even generated by the institutions of proletarian culture itself. For example, work orientations that inculcate "pride" in one's work, such as the machismo of male workers, state welfarist strategies such as pension and sickness benefits, improved working conditions that include recreational facilities, and the use of the "model worker" (Cohen and Henderson, 1991, pp. 37-40). I will extend the concept of habituation to include strategies of labour control such as restructuring of trade unions, and the state's conception of the role of trade unions in "national development", insofar as these can be seen as an attempt to gain the support or at least the acquiescence of the workers for the state defined economic goals. Even though these do not take place at the point of production, they do affect the behaviour of workers at that level. However, I hold the view that habituation cannot succeed entirely as it is often resisted by the workers through various strategies (Braverman, 1974; Crisp, 1984; Cohen and Henderson, 1991).

Restructuring and control: the early phase

When Botswana became independent in 1966, there were only four registered trade unions: the Francistown African Employees Union (FAEU), the Bechuanaland Protectorate Workers' Unions (BPWU), the Bechuanaland Trade Union Congress

(BTUC) and the Bechuanaland General Workers' Organisation (BGWO). These trade unions were split on ideological lines. The first two trade unions supported the BDP and the other two were aligned to the BPP. The pro-BDP trade unions were more inclined to pure and simple trade unionism, whilst the pro-BPP trade unions espoused a more radical nationalist line (Motshidisi, 1975). The squabbles within the trade union movement continued to fester and by 1968 there were about 20 splinter unions with only a handful registered under the Trade Unions and Trade Disputes Proclamation. According to Motshidisi (1975), most of these unions existed in name only and the whole trade union movement had degenerated into what he called "personal fiefdoms".

In 1968 there was an outbreak of spontaneous wildcat strike actions and work stoppages in places such as Francistown, Lobatse, and Gaborone. More than twenty of these industrial actions were recorded in a period of two years. The major ones involved meat workers in Lobatse and government manual workers in Gaborone. Most of the grievances were about alleged unfair dismissals, unfair labour practices and racial discrimination.[1] As I have noted in Chapter 4, at this time most businesses in Botswana were owned by either Indians or whites. Trade union consciousness therefore took the form of antiracist protests.

These strike waves must have sensitised the postcolonial state to the inadequacy of the existing labour legislation (Kirby, 1990). To begin with, the state found itself faced with a myriad of organisations and union leaders in any trade dispute. These waves of industrial action and the political factionalism within the trade union movement prompted the state to take its first steps to regulate labour by introducing two labour laws, the Trade Disputes Act and the Trade Unions Act. The two acts were enacted to "make provisions for the registration and control of trade unions".[2] The Trade Disputes Act laid down new procedures for settlement of disputes and defined circumstances under which a legal strike could occur. The Trade Unions Act introduced the concept of industrial unionism and stipulated a number of conditions to be met before a trade union could be registered and become a legal organisation. Among these conditions were that if a union that represents similar interests already exists and has been registered, no other union can be registered. The act also gave registered trade unions automatic right of recognition if 30 workers or at least 25 per cent of the labour force in the same trade or calling should want to form a union. As a result of this act most of the unions were forced to amalgamate in order to meet the requirements of the new act, and some simply withered away (Motshidisi, 1975). By October 1971 only eight of the original 30 unions remained. These were the Botswana Bank Employees Union (BBEU), the Botswana Commercial and General Workers' Union (BCGWU), the Botswana Local Government Workers' Union (BLGWU), the Botswana Meat Industries Workers' Union (BMIWU), the Botswana Construction Workers' Union (BCWU), the Botswana Mine Workers' Union (BMWU), the Botswana Railway Workers' Union (BRWU) and the National Union of Government Manual Workers' (NUGMW).

All these unions, except the BCGWU, were restructured as horizontal industrial unions in line with the requirements of the new act (Motshidisi, 1975; Frimpong and Olsen, 1985). Only the BCGWU, which organised in the hotel, retail and wholesale sector, was allowed to remain a general union. The restructuring of trade unions along industrial lines and the increased state control of trade unions were similar to the measures taken against the trade unions in other developing nations like Zambia, Kenya and Ghana. The important point to note is that these countries were one party states, or in the case of Ghana, had a military government. But notwithstanding the differences in the form of government, the actions of the postcolonial state in these countries were very similar. In Botswana, as was the case in these countries, it was the fragmented nature and enterprise orientation of the colonial period that made it difficult for the state to exercise any control over multiple trade unions. The state responded by restructuring and consolidating trade unions in order to maximise its control and influence in the trade union movement.

However, in Botswana, these measures did not completely eradicate the trade union ideological rivalry of the pre-Independence era. In January 1968, the Commissioner of Labour (who was also the Registrar of Trade Unions), Mr P. Mmusi called a meeting of all registered trade unions in Botswana.[3] At this meeting the Commissioner of Labour argued that the continued existence of ideological rivalries in the trade union movement was indicative of a lack of elementary trade union education on the part of the workers. It was decided by the government, through the Commissioner of Labour, that trade a union education programme should be started without any delay (Motshidisi, 1975). To this end, a labour education committee - the National Labour Training Committee, was set up with G.M.K. Mmusi, a representative of the Bechuanaland Federation of Labour (BFL), as its chairman, and K. Motshidisi, a representative of the BTUC, as the secretary. The Committee was also requested by the Commissioner of Labour to look into the question of unity in the labour movement. It was resolved that unity talks between the BTUC and the BFL should be initiated. But while efforts were still under way to find an internal solution, the government sought and received technical assistance from the American African Labour Centre (AALC) (Frimpong and Olsen, 1985).

In 1971, the AALC gave funds for the construction of the Botswana Trade Union Education Centre (BTUEC) offices. The centre, which was staffed by AALC technical advisers, was charged with the responsibility of organising a trade union educational programme and working towards the establishment of one national centre. Thus the AALC technical assistance effectively removed the task of rebuilding the trade union movement from the indigenous people. Between 1972 and 1974, over 2,000 trade unionists participated in seminars and workshops organised under the auspices of this project (Molutsi et al., 1992). One other area of AALC involvement in Botswana, like elsewhere in the Third World, was through "leadership training" courses in the United States, and several members of the BFTU executive committees went to the United States for a variety of trade union leadership courses. The AALC's budget for trade union education for Botswana for the year ended 1975 was US$61,275 (Thompson and Larson, 1978).

Restructuring and control: the later phase

The state also exerted considerable pressure on the trade unions to come together in a federation. For instance in 1971, Seretse Khama, the first President of Botswana, argued very strongly for the restructuring of the trade unions in Botswana. Speaking at the ceremony to mark the opening of the BTUEC, he stressed the need for a central body representing all registered trade unions in Botswana. He argued:

> This should eliminate the dangers of rival unions competing against each other in destructive militancy and not protecting the interests of their members in a responsible way. The existence of industrial unions should also help to eliminate the damaging personal rivalries which used to handicap trade union development.[4]

It was only in 1977 that the trade union movement came together to form a federation - the BFTU. Unlike in countries such as Zambia, Kenya, and Ghana, the formation of the national centre was not imposed by the state, nor was it made compulsory for trade unions in Botswana to affiliate to the BFTU. In fact the BFTU initially comprised only four trade unions: the BRWU, the BMWU, the BBEU and the Diamond Sorters and Valuators Union (BDVU). However this apparently liberal policy does not depart from the main argument that the creation of the BFTU was a form of state control envisaged by the state, as the following discussion will elucidate.

The formation of the first BFTU executive committee in 1977 saw a power struggle between the remnants of BFL and BTUC. A former secretary general of BFTU has pointed out that he and his colleagues had for some time suspected that AALC and the Friedrich Ebert Foundation (FEF) were secretly involved in lobbying and funding the elections for the positions of the chairman and secretary general of the new federation.[5] It would seem that some members of the ruling BDP, the AALC and the FEF, especially one J. Helfer, who was the AALC chief representative for Botswana, Lesotho and Swaziland, and a Dr Adams, the FEF representative in Botswana (who was also rumoured to be a political adviser to the ruling BDP), were worried by the influence of radical elements from the BTUC. According to Mabiletsa, there were rumours that the BDP-AALC-FEF circle had a slate of candidates for the BFTU leadership and that the top jobs in the federation, that of the national chairman and the secretary general, were earmarked for BDP leaning unionists, namely Gaotlhaetse Matlhabaphiri and Pelotelele Tlhaodi. After some intense lobbying, the BDP candidates got the jobs. This victory by the pro-BDP unionists led to another round of power struggle as the radicals resurrected the old rivalries and campaigned among the rank and file members against the two. Matlhabaphiri was at this time the chairman of the BDVU. Within about six months of the election of the BFTU executive committee, the federation almost split up, with the rank and file members saying that they did not want BDP activists leading the federation, and by mid 1978, there were two secretary generals, namely Tlhaodi from the BDP-AALC-FEF camp, and Ditiro Saleshando - from the more radical faction.

The problem continued to fester until the end of the Matlhabaphiri and Tlhaodi term of office in 1980, when the radical faction amended the BFTU's Constitution, removing the clauses that prohibited them from electing their leadership in full freedom, and elected a new executive.[6] However, the Registrar of Trade Unions refused to recognise the new executive on a technicality, saying that the elections were illegal because they were carried out before the amendments to the BFTU's Constitution were notified to the registrar as required by the Trade Unions Act. New elections were held, and Ronald Baipidi was chosen as a compromise secretary general. Matlhabaphiri later became a specially elected Member of Parliament and Tlhaodi became a specially elected councillor in the Gaborone Town Council.

Having delineated some of the problems that bedeviled Botswana's trade union movement in the immediate postcolonial years, and the efforts of the postcolonial petty bourgeois state elite to increase its control of the labour movement, I now turn to the role played by some international labour organisations. This is important since their ideological position gives us clues about trade unionism in Botswana and has implications for the direction of the trade union movement in the country. There are at the moment three international trade union organisations operating in Botswana. These are the International Confederation of Free Trade Unions (ICFTU) - a trade union international whose regional head office is in Harare, the AALC and the FEF (this German organisation is linked to the German Social Democratic Party).[7] The ICFTU is not very active in the day to day affairs of the BFTU. The most active of these organisations today are the AALC and the FEF.

The role of the AALC in the trade union movement in Botswana and in the Third World trade unions should be examined within the context of the cold war rivalry that plagued the international trade union movement. As Thompson and Larson (1978) argue, the Third World unions have been a site of clashes and rivalry between the American Federation of Labour-Central Industrial Organisations (AFL-CIO), and the ICFTU for the control of Third World trade unions. Horbart Spalding, a researcher on the foreign policy of the American labour movement has argued that:

... the AFL-CIO foreign policy flows from its domestic positions. Abroad, it combats anticapitalist ideologies and organisations and it aids and encourages procapitalist unions. It attempts to influence existing unions and to form new ones in its own image. Where interests overlap, it works with US corporations, and in close cooperation with their representatives in the government. Disagreements between business and labour bureaucracy in foreign policy matters, as in internal affairs, stem from tactical questions, and not from philosophical antagonisms (p. 2).

73

Thompson and Larson (1978) quote George Meaney, a long time head of the AFL-CIO remarking that "We are not about to trade in our system for any other", that he believes in capitalism, that he is a member of a capitalist society and is dedicated to the preservation of the capitalist system which, he argued, rewards workers. According to Thompson and Larson, the AFL-CIO operates in Africa through its Africa arm, the AALC. They argue that the AALC seems to have got the upper hand, while the ICFTU has had many doors slammed in its face, because of the accusation that it is linked to the Central Intelligence Agency (CIA). They argue that in fact it is the AALC which is linked to the agency. Thompson and Larson argue that the AALC has been able to glide with consummate ease through several countries, because it has money, political support from the State Department, and a way of organising trade unions "that appeals to governments not noted for their affection towards workers movements" (Thompson and Larson, 1978, p. 48).

Ideological habituation

Having described the processes of restructuring trade unions and retraining trade union leaders as forms of state control I turn now to another form of trade union control which can be characterised as ideological habituation. This involves the manipulation of trade unions through the ideology of "national interest" or "national development". This form of control is instilled through persuasion or ideological manipulation. Here the state or its representatives attempt to present the interests of capital as the common interests of all and attempt to persuade the working class to accept the system of unequal distribution of the products of their labour. By so doing the state or the petty bourgeois state elite try to adjust the workers to the labour process in its capitalist form. Ideological habituation, unlike other forms of control such as restructuring which involve an element of legal coercion, is a form of labour control which functions predominantly by ideology. It seeks to maximise surplus value extraction by making the workers accept the system of unequal distribution of the products of their labour for a reason such as "national development". It can be directed at the individual worker, at a group of workers or at the whole working class. Thus for the most part of the postcolonial period the labour movement in Botswana has been reminded time and time again of its responsibility to the nation. The petty bourgeois state elite, specifically President Khama and his cabinet colleagues, have on various occasions stressed the need for "wages restraint", "industrial peace" and "political stability" in order to achieve "national development".

This perception of the role of trade unions in development was first articulated by Seretse Khama in July 1971. The President mentioned that while his government recognised that trade unions had a role to play in participatory democracy, workers had to realise that they had the responsibility to assist the development of the country. President Khama argued:

74

We in Botswana have given trade unions freedom to represent their members' interests and guide the aspirations of our workers so that they make a productive contribution to national growth ... In return we expect the trade unions and their officials to recognise that their contribution must be made through these channels and not by direct involvement in the political arena ... Equally workers must recognise that if we are to attract industry to Botswana in order to assist our development, and create jobs for our people, we must make sure that the investment offers a reasonable return.[8]

The President pointed out that workers were in the minority and should exercise the freedom to bargain collectively carefully, bearing in mind their responsibility to the nation as a whole. According to him, freedom carries with it responsibility: "Your first responsibility is to assist in the development of the country. This is the first responsibility of all *Batswana*."

Again when he officially opened the Orapa Diamond Mine in 1972, the President pointed out that workers must understand that the "objective of an organised labour movement is not just to promote the narrow interests of its members", but rather it has "a responsibility to the nation as a whole".[9] In his address to the Selebi Phikwe mine workers, two months after Botswana's most violent strike, the President had this to say:

Botswana is a poor and underdeveloped country. We all agree hat this is so. And I am sure we all agree that in order for meaningful economic development to take place in the country, in an orderly fashion, there is a need for industrial peace and political stability ... Even our Independence was considered premature in 1966 since we did not have an industrial base from which to develop our economy and thus ensure our survival as a nation ... It is well to remind you that as a young developing country we will for many years depend to a large degree on external assistance for development funds. This assistance cannot continue unless we maintain peace and stability in our country. Botswana would lose its reputation as a stable and safe country thereby scaring away investors ... if every time there is some grievance among workers, rioting takes place with no regard whatsoever to the legal machinery provided for settling disputes peacefully and amicably.[10]

Again in 1977, at the first delegates conference of the BFTU, Seretse Khama told the delegates:

You do not live in isolation from the rest of the country and its economic realities. Like government, you have a wider responsibility ... you are first and foremost *Batswana*, and your first responsibility is to assist in the development of the country.[11]

Cabinet ministers have also argued on various occasions that workers must recognise that if the country is to attract foreign investment to assist in national development and create jobs, and if investors are to be persuaded to come to Botswana rather than go elsewhere, Botswana must make it worth their while by ensuring that their investments offer a reasonable return. Ministers have also exhorted workers to work hard, be disciplined and exercise restraint on wages demands and follow legal channels in the pursuance of industrial disputes, and avoid unnecessary strike actions. They have argued that workers are a minority and should not demand more than their fair share of the country's wealth in wages, that workers must not hold the country hostage by illegal strike actions, and that trade unions must be responsible organisations that respect the rule of law.[12]

Chapter 3 gave an account of the role of the state in fostering the economic growth of the country and Chapter 4 examined some of the policies adopted by the state towards that end. One such policy was the policy on wages. As indicated above, this policy was structured in such a way that it virtually ruled out collective bargaining as the mechanism of wages determination in a market economy.[13] The critical question is, if it was solely diamond mining revenues that were responsible for Botswana's economic development, and not low wages policy, what would have been the point all these exhortations by the petty bourgeois state elite on the need for wages restraint and industrial peace? What would have been the point of clinging to a policy that to all intents and purposes was redundant? It is argued here that the low wages policy was never redundant or even made temporarily irrelevant by the diamond boom. The wages policy has always been used to control and hold down wages even during the period of the diamond boom. The fact that the policy has never lost its relevance is acknowledged by the ruling party and the government; this point was underscored by Minister Kwelagobe in a speech at the delegates conference of BFTU. According to the minister:

> One reason why we ... have been able to sustain this [economic] growth ... and for this the trade union movement must take a lot of the credit - has been the implementation of a policy of wages restraint. This policy does restrict the ability of unions to bargain freely with employers. We have never pretended otherwise. It is, if you like, government interference in the freedom of collective bargaining. Despite this restriction on legitimate trade union aspirations, you have, I believe, understood and appreciated the economic reasons behind the policy, and it is to your credit that most workers in Botswana now accept the policy ... I do not think there are many countries in the world where workers would accept a total pay freeze with the understanding which the trade unions and workers of Botswana [have] expressed ... and an appreciation of the economic conditions which made the pay freeze necessary.[14]

Minister Kwelagobe pointed out that though his party supports a strong trade union movement, the interests of the workers should not take precedence over what he called the interests of the country as a whole, and that the trade unions should develop a role which meets the needs of the country and should not adopt what he termed "an imported trade union philosophy with its folk history and perceptions built up over years of strife in Europe".

The other factor that points to the centrality of wage labour in Botswana's development concerns labour productivity. There has been in the last few years an orchestrated campaign by the state and employers accusing workers of low productivity.[15] What I wish to point out, without going into all the arguments for and against this accusation, is that it is not surprising that it is labour productivity and not world markets that should be singled out and blamed. This supports the argument that it was a low wages policy, and not diamonds per se, that played a crucial role in the postcolonial economic development. It is a point well worth noting because even in the third phase of Botswana's development, the petty bourgeois state elite still maintains that Botswana must continue to seek foreign investment as well as overseas aid to provide for all the capital required to achieve economic growth. The government has argued that such investment can only be attracted to the country if it is permitted a rate of return not less favourable than normally obtainable elsewhere, and that the basis of a policy of wages restraint would be vitiated if the level of taxation on profits in Botswana was raised to a point at which no investor would benefit from the comparative advantages offered in Botswana.

Conclusion

The foregoing discussion has examined the various forms of state control of the working class. After Independence, the state embarked on a systematic programme of restructuring the trade union movement to maximise the state control on trade unions and make the workers acquiescent and supportive of the state defined economic policies. To this end the postcolonial petty bourgeois state elite created a corporate nationalist model in which wages restraint for national development became the rallying cry. Lack of development in the colonial era served as a powerful reminder to the workers that wages restraint is in the "national interest" and that workers had to accept sacrifice. As pointed out, habituation is also a process that involves interior determination, that is, a process of transmitting the elements of culture that are even generated by the institutions of the proletarian culture itself. Habituation as a form of ideological control presupposes consent. The critical aim of class analysis is to reveal relations of domination and subordination often concealed by false explanations and justifications perpetuated by the state elite to sustain the process of accumulation (Zeitlin, 1980). To the extent that these false explanations and justifications are accepted by the working class, the petty bourgeois state elite would have achieved class hegemony by consent. But consent of the dominated can sometimes be eroded or subverted by the counter ideologies of the working class. As Zeitlin points out, class hegemony cannot rest on consent of the exploited alone, but also requires coercion. This is ultimately the indispensable means of class domination because without it consent can be withdrawn. In the field of industrial relations this coercion appears in the form of labour law. This is the point to which I now turn.

Notes

1   *The Botswana Daily News* (19 January 1968, 19 August 1968, 23 August 1968 and 24 August 1968).

2   See the *Preamble to the Trade Unions and Trade Disputes Act Amendment Bill* (1968).

3   Peter Mmusi was later to become Botswana's Vice President, and chairman of the ruling party. In this he had followed some other African politicians like Tom Mboya of Kenya, Rashid Kawawa of Tanzania and even Sekou Toure of Guinea, who used trade union movement as a stepping stone to political office. Peter Mmusi resigned in disgrace from both the government and the chairmanship of the BDP, following a scandal on abuse of office.

4   Seretse Khama's speech at the BTUEC opening ceremony, 10 July 1971.

5   Interview with Isaac Mabiletsa, 30 August 1991.

6   Ibid.

7   The FEF always maintained very strong links with the ruling BDP and has supported the party financially for about twenty years. In 1988, a BDP administrator was found guilty of embezzling about P80,000 donated to the party under his name.

8   Seretse Khama's speech on 10 July 1971. The ceremony was also attended by two senior AALC officials - Mr Patrick O'Farrell, AALC deputy director general based in Geneva, and Mr Gerry Frank, AALC regional director based in Addis Ababa, Ethiopia.

9   Seretse Khama's speech at Orapa, 26 May 1972.

10   Seretse Khama to workers in Selebi Phikwe, 19 December 1975.

11   Seretse Khama's speech at the inauguration of First Delegates' Conference of the BFTU, 2 April 1977.

12   See a compilation of several speeches of Botswana cabinet ministers - *Why We Need An Incomes Policy, Ministers Speak,* Botswana Government Printer (not dated), and also *The Role of Workers and Trade Unions in Botswana,* a compilation of speeches by B.K. Kgari, a minister responsible for labour in the 1970s.

13   See the keynote address to the seminar on the revision of the Employment Act and the Trade Disputes Act, by T. Lebang, Commissioner of Labour, Ministry of Labour and Social Security, 27 August 1990.

14   See the address by Daniel Kwelagobe to the BFTU Delegates Conference, 23 June 1984. Before his political downfall, this minister was perhaps the most powerful man in Botswana after the President. He was the secretary general of the ruling BDP and also the Minister of Public Service and Information. This ministry, which is now called the Ministry of Presidential Affairs and Public Administration, is responsible for the Botswana state apparatus, the army, the police, and the civil service. The ministry also controls the state owned Radio Botswana and *The Botswana Daily News* tabloid.

15   See *Working Harder for Botswana* (1985), a report on the National Seminar on Labour Productivity, University of Botswana: Gaborone.

6 Labour law and industrial relations

Introduction

This chapter analyses labour legislation and its impact on the development of the country's industrial relations system. The chapter traces the process from the time of Independence in 1966 until 1990, when the state abandoned two decades of direct intervention in the economy and in the industrial relations scene. It is argued that the industrial relations system that emerged after Independence was characterised by the state's domination and subordination of labour. This represented a system of labour repression that has often been concealed by Botswana's liberal democratic Constitution and commitment to individual rights and freedoms. The industrial relations system must be viewed within the context of the country's policy of economic growth based on private capital accumulation and foreign capital investment. Although trade unions in Botswana were legalised in 1942 by the Trade Unions and Trade Disputes Proclamation, the country still had no established industrial relations system at Independence (Kirby, 1990).

The gradual expansion in formal sector employment created the need to bring together some aspects of common law affecting the employment relationship up to date, and a new law, the Employment Act No. 15 of 1963, was enacted to replace the old Master and Servants Act (Kirby, 1990). The Trade Union and Trades Disputes Proclamation (1942) and the Employment Act of 1963 remained the main labour laws until 1969. Kirby (1990) points out that at the time of Independence there was still no machinery for the settlement of trade disputes, and the 1942 trade union legislation was woefully inadequate. As a result, in 1969 the Trade Unions Act No. 24/1969 and the Trade Disputes Act No. 28/1969 were enacted to replace the outdated legislation of 1942. These were Botswana's introduction to modern labour legislation. But with the rapid development of new industries in the various sectors of the economy, these laws were perceived to be inadequate. In June 1983 a comprehensive and updated Trade Disputes Act was enacted and was followed in 1984 by the revamped Employment Act and the Trade Unions and Employers'

Organisations Act. In 1992, these laws were again amended and the Industrial Court was created. Three of these pieces of legislation that will be considered here. These are (a) the Employment Act, (b) the Trade Unions and Employers' Organisations Act and (c) the Trade Disputes Act. Since Botswana is a formally liberal democratic country, and it is on the country's Constitution that its statute law is based, any analysis of Botswana's labour laws must begin with an examination of the country's constitutional provisions on labour issues. It is argued here that Botswana's labour laws, which constitute a system of labour repression, are predicated on the Constitution of the country which guarantees fundamental rights and freedoms of individuals but restricts these rights and freedoms in the case of labour organisations.

The Constitution and labour legislation

The Constitution that paved the way for Independence in September 1966 guaranteed and protected the fundamental rights and freedoms of the individual. These rights and freedoms include the right to personal liberty, protection from deprivation of property, freedom of conscience and expression, and freedom of assembly and association. In particular Section 13(1) of the Constitution states that:

> Except with his own consent, no person shall be hindered in the enjoyment of his freedom of assembly and association, that is to say, his right to assemble freely and associate with other persons and in particular to form or belong to trade unions or other associations for the protection of his interests.

However, these rights and freedoms only apply to individuals and have been restricted in the case of labour organisations. That is to say, though the Constitution guarantees the individual's right to form and belong to a trade union, the rights and freedoms of the trade unions have been restricted whilst the rights of the individual who may belong to such trade unions are left untrammelled. This was made possible by a constitutional amendment which followed a wave of illegal and wildcat strike actions across the country. In April 1969 the Parliament amended the original 1966 Constitution to include a subsection restricting the rights and freedoms of trade unions. According to the 1969 amendment, Section 13(2a) of the 1966 Independence Order was reformulated to read that "no law that imposes *restrictions* upon public officers, employees of local government bodies or teachers shall be held to be inconsistent with the provisions of Section 13(1)", and a new section -Section 13(2d) was added. The additional part stipulates that "a law can be formulated that makes provision for the registration of trade unions and imposes *reasonable conditions* relating to the requirements for registration".[1]

The effect of this is that Botswana's Constitution guarantees individual rights and freedoms, but restricts collective rights and freedoms, especially as they apply to the labour movement. These restrictions on the constitutional rights of trade unions were political and intended to control the trade unions, make them toe the line and create propitious conditions for capital accumulation in line with the postcolonial state's objective of rapid a economic growth capitalist strategy. In a way this was consistent with an emerging trend in the newly independent African countries whereby measures to deal with trade unions and reform the industrial relations system were now common. This new approach seems to have been motivated by the desire by the ruling petty bourgeois elite to protect itself from organised labour as a source of opposition, as well as the need to neutralise the labour movement as the centre of opposition to the new economic and social policies that were envisaged by the new rulers (Gladstone, 1980).

In 1969, just three years after Independence, the new government decided to revise the labour laws. Leading the debate on the proposed amendments, the Minister of Health, Labour and Social Services argued that the government should have the powers to restrict the activities of workers, especially those in the public sector because they are paid by the state. But it is interesting to note that although the amendment was ostensibly for public sector employees, it carried a provision that laws can be formulated that "impose reasonable conditions relating to the registration of trade unions." In fact it was at the same sitting of the Parliament in the aftermath of the 1968 wave of strikes that the process to overhaul Botswana's labour laws started.[2]

The amendment was opposed by the only two opposition Members of Parliament, Mr P.G.Matante and Mr T.W.Motlhagodi, but even then on the grounds that it discriminated against the trade unions specifically, and not other voluntary organisations like political parties and women's and youth organisations. In his reply, the minister argued that:

> [Whilst] other voluntary organisations contributed to the social progress of the country, they did not have the same potential for building up or breaking down the economy of the country such as trade unions had, and that is why all over the world, governments controlled the formation and running of the trade unions while they took no such interest in the political, women's and youth organisations.[3]

In that month alone, in addition to passing this constitutional amendment, Parliament also enacted three amendments to the labour laws: the Trade Unions Act of 1969, the Trade Disputes Act of 1969 and the Regulation of Wages and Conditions of Employment Act of 1969. The Parliament also passed the Public Service Act which governed the conditions of service of the public sector employees. Reacting to criticism from trade union leaders that they had not been consulted, the minister was very blunt and forthright in his reply:

> Representative democracy, as against the popular type, provides for delegating legislative responsibility to few people who may consult the electorate, follow some or none of its views as they find fit, which we have done in this

particular case and that generally as elected leaders of people, we are not going to follow people all the time, but must lead them.[4]

In effect, these laws replaced the Trades Unions and Trade Disputes Proclamation (1942) and the Employment Law No. 15/1963 and marked the beginning of Botswana's own industrial relations system.

The Employment Act

The Employment Act is the basic labour law of Botswana and provides the so called floor of rights, that is, the statutory employment rights for individuals at work. The act replaced the Regulation of Wages and Conditions of Employment Act (1969). The act defines, guarantees and protects conditions of employment. These include contracts of employment, rest periods, hours of work, overtime, public holidays, annual leave, employment of females, children and young persons and the infirm and the handicapped, establishment of labour health areas, sick leave, determination of minimum wages, redundancy procedures. The law specifies remedies, jurisdiction, procedures and penalties in respect of matters pertaining to the infringement of the act. It covers all employees in the country except the public sector employees and domestic and agricultural workers, who are not defined as employees for the purpose of the act.[5] The act defines an employee as any individual who has entered into a contract of employment for hire of his labour, provided that the expression *does not* include a *public officer* or a person employed by a local authority unless he belongs to the industrial class. According to the act the term "employer" applies to government only in respect of any of its officers or servants who belong to a category of such officers or servants the members of which are declared by the regulations to be employees for the purposes of the act.

In an attempt to give effect to Section 13(1) of the Constitution, the act restricts employers from terminating employees' job contracts as a result of their membership of a registered trade union and/or for any reason which could be interpreted as discriminatory on the basis of colour, creed or ethnic origin. Before the 1992 amendments, Section 26 of the act gave the employer the right to terminate a contract of employment without notice, where the employee was guilty of "serious misconduct". The trade unions felt that the employers abused the clause to get rid of "trouble makers" in the work force. The 1992 amendments defined "serious misconduct" more precisely. Section 27 of the act gave both the employer and the employee the right to protest against termination of employment by either party to the contract of employment. Under this section, the labour officer had the powers to investigate cases involving termination of contract of employment by either party to the contract, and to order reinstatement in cases of unfair dismissals. The employers argued that they were being forced to retain workers who were unproductive. This section was repealed by the 1992 amendment. According to the revised law, allegations of unfair dismissals will be decided by the Industrial Court.

Trade Unions and Employers' Organisations Act (1984)

This act replaced the Trade Unions Act of 1969. The act provides procedures for registration, recognition and ultimately control and supervision of trade unions by the state. It is only when trade unions have been duly registered and issued with a certificate of registration that they become lawful and legal organisations. Once a trade union is registered, the trade union and its officers and members enjoy trade union rights and immunities and privileges conferred by Section 17 of the act. The section stipulates that no suit or other legal proceedings shall be maintainable in any civil court against the registered trade union or any of its officers or members in respect of any act done in furtherance of a trade dispute. According to Section 17 of the act:

> ... no suit against the registered trade union or any officer or member thereof on behalf of himself and all other members of the trade union in respect of any delictual act alleged to have been committed by or on behalf of the trade union shall be entertained by any court;

and

> ... the objects of the registered trade union shall not, by reason only that they are in restraint of trade, be unlawful so as to render

> (i) any member of the trade union liable to criminal prosecution, or

> (ii) void or voidable any agreement or trust.

Once a trade union has been registered by the state and issued with a certificate of registration it becomes the recognised trade union for that particular industry, and it does not have to negotiate for recognition with the employer. Section 50 of the act compels the employer to deal with that trade union as a negotiating body, and any employer who fails to negotiate with a registered trade union or its branch is guilty of an offence. However, the duty to recognise a trade union arises only if the membership of the union is 25 per cent or more of the employees in that industry.

On the face of it, this is a very generous allowance to trade unionism, especially by Third World standards. But a closer reading of the act reveals that in practice trade union rights and freedoms in Botswana are severely restricted. The act actually contains a variety of labour control measures and restrictions on the rights and freedoms of trade unions. For example, Section 10 of the act gives the Registrar of Trade Unions the power to refuse to register a trade union and to cancel the registration of a registered trade union for a number of reasons. For instance registration of a trade union can be refused if one of its principal officers has been convicted of an offence under the act or under the Trade Disputes Act, or if the registrar is satisfied that any of its principal officers is not a citizen of Botswana. Another mechanism of trade union control which interferes with the freedom of a registered trade union organisation, concerns the rights, immunities and privileges conferred by Section 17 of the act. Although once registered, a trade union enjoys certain rights, immunities and privileges, these extend to trade union officers and members only, but not to the people in full time employment of the trade unions - that is, the full time administrators or employees of the trade unions.

Yet another control mechanism is contained in Section 21 and in Section 22 of the act which restrict membership of the trade union. According to Section 21, no person shall be admitted to membership of a trade union unless he is an employee in an industry with which the trade union is directly concerned, and that an employee of a trade union cannot be a member of that trade union, and that a member of a trade union who becomes an employee of the trade union shall cease to be a member of the trade union. Before the 1992 amendment, the act stipulated that a member of a trade union who had ceased to be an employee, should also cease to be a member of that trade union. In 1992 this section was amended to allow a worker to remain a member of a trade union whilst his or her case was still on appeal. The worker will still cease to be a member if he loses the appeal. Section 22 of the act stipulates who qualifies to become an officer of a trade union. According to the act, no person can become an officer of a trade union or a federation of trade unions unless that person is a member of the trade union or of a trade union belonging to the federation of trade unions.

These two sections are of particular importance in the state control of the unions. In the first place, these sections of the act effectively prevent the trade unions, and the trade unions federation, the BFTU, from having full time officials. The BFTU and the national unions can only have as full time staff, *employees* who are not entitled to the enjoyment of the rights, immunities and privileges conferred by Section 17 of the act. What this means is that trade unions, from a branch to a national union and up to the BFTU, cannot have full time officials. They can only have *employees*, who do not enjoy rights, immunities and privileges accorded to trade unionists under Section 17 of the act. These people are regarded as *employees*, and not *officials* or even members of the trade union they are working for, and as employees, as opposed to officials or members, they do not enjoy the immunities, rights and privileges granted by Section 17. The previous secretary general of the BFTU, Ronald Baipidi, articulated the problems of the BFTU in these words:

> ... BFTU and the national unions are run on a part time basis because that is what the law says. They (the government) know that it is logistically impossible for us to meet every time we want to meet, because members of the executive committees are spread all over the country. We are expected to conduct our affairs by telephone, and even then after hours. The BFTU's full time staff have no political mandate. It is the part time officials who have the

mandate. But we are expected to be at our places of employment during normal working hours. Unlike the employers' organisations, union employees cannot make decisions on behalf of the BFTU. They cannot vote for or against a proposal because they have no political mandate. Those with the mandate like the secretary general are full time employees elsewhere and often are not available to decide on important matters at the right time. We attend executive committee meetings after hours, when we leave our place of employment. This part time work for the union does not give the officials the time they require to attend to union or BFTU business. You must also understand that these people have family commitments after work. It is either the unions which suffer or it is the family that suffers.[6]

The state's restrictions on the rights and freedoms of the trade unions stands in sharp contrast to the absence of such interference in the employers' organisations. There are no restrictions on membership of the employers' organisations nor does the state prescribe to them the type of office bearers they can or cannot have. To begin with most employers in Botswana are expatriates, and secondly, though the employers' organisation, the Botswana Confederation of Commerce, Industry and Manpower (BOCCIM), has a local director and a deputy director, it is largely run by expatriate staff or "technical advisers" from abroad. According to sources inside the BFTU, BOCCIM is really run by the expatriates who do the technical or specialist jobs, while the local director and his deputy are just used to rubber stamp and execute the decisions. As Ronald Baipidi puts it:

Our labour laws are repressive, and pro-employer. We are not allowed to request money from outside the country, yet employers are not likewise restricted. That organisation is run by employers who are not citizens of the country. We are not allowed to have the assistance of noncitizens, but BOCCIM is staffed by expatriates. Its local director is a figurehead. All technical experts are American or British.[7]

Although these may be dismissed as subjective views which cannot be verified, one is struck by BOCCIM's highly qualified expatriate staff and financial resources and by the extent of the involvement of foreign capital in the affairs of BOCCIM. But this is to be expected, because after all the state is committed to attracting foreign capital to Botswana, and it is quite possible that such foreign capital will come only on certain terms, including the right to run their affairs in their own way. That capital should be allowed the rights and freedoms that are not available to labour indicates that the state is never neutral in a class divided society. As I have pointed out already, under conditions of private capital accumulation, the state, although appearing to be standing above the fray of class antagonisms, in reality serves the long term interests of capital.

The provisions of the act that have been examined here show how the state has been able to control labour and keep the trade unions organisationally weak while allowing the employers' organisations a relatively free hand. However, according to one government minister, there is nothing wrong with the act. Addressing the 1984 BFTU delegates' conference, the Secretary General of the ruling BDP, Mr Kwelagobe, said that he saw no way in which the act infringed on what he called the "legitimate concerns and interests" of the trade union movement, and that the legislation was there to ensure the "orderly development" and administration of trade unions. He further stated that:

We in the party have always felt strongly that economic development in Botswana is a partnership between government, employers and workers. We see the role of government as providing a suitable environment to promote development and the necessary ventures to attract investment.[8]

Addressing himself to the organisational problems posed by these legal restrictions, Minister Kwelagobe defended the government position by arguing that there is a general principle of separating policy issues from implementation issues. He argued:

... the same principle of divorcing the implementation of decisions applies in government. Members of Parliament and ministers are charged with the responsibility of establishing a policy and the civil service has the responsibility of implementing such policy. A permanent secretary doesn't have to be a minister in order to implement government policy. He still remains a permanent secretary and his job is to implement the policy which has been formulated or fashioned by the Parliament and the ministers.[9]

A Gaborone based labour consultant was even more sympathetic to the government view. During an interview he said that he thought that the trade unionists are using Section 17 as a "red herring" and argued that the BFTU is not the only organisation with a split between policy and administration. He argued that the difference between officials and employees of the BFTU is that officials can vote whereas employees cannot, but that they are all free to participate in BFTU activities. He pointed out:

To say that Section 17 of the act is discriminating and weakens the labour movement is not true. I know that they (trade unionists) always say that. This is just a red herring. Most organisations in Botswana, including the ruling party, clearly differentiate between administration and policy making. The BDP policy makers are employed elsewhere as ministers, and they only run the party on part time basis. I think the problem with the BFTU is the calibre of their manpower. Contrast it with the Botswana Mine Workers' Union. It is really strong because of the calibre of people like Saleshando and Setlhare. But the union is run on part time basis. The chairman and the secretary

87

general are both full time employees of BCL [Bamangwato Concessions Ltd].[10]

There is some truth in the argument that there is a difference between policy and implementation. But whether the BFTU should be able to function efficiently without full time officials is debatable. In the first instance, the issue is that the state has created structures for the labour movement and the labour movement is not happy with those structures. In the view of the trade unions, these structures prevent the trade unions from organising in the way that they as the labour movement feel is most effective. It is the state, and not trade unions themselves, which has prescribed ways on how the labour movement should organise. This is the central issue raised by the BFTU. To argue that policy must be separated from implementation and administration, does not in any way invalidate the arguments raised by the BFTU, let alone lessen the repressive nature of the act. The bottom line is that the trade unions do not organise in the manner and methods chosen by themselves, but in the manner and method prescribed to them by the state. This is a form of labour repression and interference with the right of labour to organise in full freedom. In any case there is very little basis to compare the BFTU officials to government ministers. It is not true that ministers are responsible for policy formulation. The policies are the responsibility of the party and of the Parliament. Ministers are appointed to go and implement these policies, and to do this they rely on the state civil bureaucracy. At the same time the ministers and the permanent secretaries are paid from the national coffers, and not by the party. The state and the employers command resources that the BFTU does not have.

Another mechanism of control that was repealed by the 1992 amendments was Section 30 of the act. This section empowered the minister to send a representative to the meetings of the BFTU's executive committee. According to the act, the minister could send a representative to attend every meeting of the body in which the ultimate authority of the BFTU is vested, that is, the National Council of the BFTU, which meets biennially. The minister could also send his representative to the federation's executive committee meeting. The minister's representative could take part in the deliberations of the meetings, although he could not vote. In addition to this, the Constitution of the BFTU carried a clause that recognised the attendance of the government representative. A former executive committee member of the BFTU, and now a Member of Parliament for the opposition BNF informed me:

> The BFTU Constitution has to carry a clause that recognises the government representative at conferences. You have to write to the Registrar of Trade Unions informing him of the time and date of the meeting, so that he could arrange to send a representative. Any attempts to exclude the minister's representative will render those deliberations null and void.[11]

In addition, the trade unions and the BFTU are required to furnish the Registrar of Trade Unions with the names of their office bearers, and as Mabiletsa pointed out, if the registrar can detect that one of the office bearers is not a citizen or a full time employee, he has the power to dissolve the executive committee under Section 10(3) of the act. But by contrast, this does not apply to employers' organisations. In 1994, thirteen of the twenty six members of the BOCCIM Executive Council were noncitizens, almost all of them managing directors of foreign companies doing business in Botswana. To crown all these mechanisms of control of the trade union movement, Section 32 of the act stipulated that the books containing the minutes of the proceedings of the executive committees of registered trade unions or the meetings of the body in which the ultimate authority of a registered trade unions was vested or of the executive committee of the trade union federation, were to be open for inspection by any member of the trade union or by any person authorised on that behalf by the registrar. This section was repealed by the 1992 amendments.

The Trade Disputes Act

Before the 1992 amendments, this act covered areas such as procedures for settlement of disputes, arbitration by the Permanent Arbitrator, settlement of claims and collective labour agreement, unlawful industrial action, enforcement of collective labour agreements and awards of the Permanent Arbitrator, and protection of essential services. There were two major characteristics of this act in the period up to 1992. The first was giving the state the powers to intervene at any time in any trade dispute, and the second characteristic was creating a mediation-conciliation-compulsory arbitration procedures to deal with bargaining deadlocks. Sections 4 to 11 of the Trade Disputes Act spelt out the procedures for the settlement of disputes, prescribed steps to be followed in any labour dispute, and also gave the Commissioner of Labour the power to intervene in any trade dispute, even if that dispute had not been formally reported to him. For example, Section 4(1) of the act stipulated that:

Where the Commissioner of Labour is satisfied that a trade dispute exists or is apprehended, he may, whether the dispute has or has not been reported to him under Section 5, mediate between the parties to the dispute or authorise some other person so to mediate.

The act provided the procedures and administrative framework through which disputes between employees and employers could be settled and handled. The act made provisions for a legal strike, but excluded workers in essential services (that is, electricity supply, water supply, health). Certain procedures, however, had to be followed for strikes to legally occur. The act specified that strikes (or threats of strike) could be declared illegal by the Minister of Labour and Home Affairs if in his judgement the procedures for settling a dispute had not been exhausted, or when workers wanted to strike in sympathy or in support of others, or when the strike was intended to force employers to employ only union members (the so called "closed shop"), or when the issue at hand is in the hands of the Permanent Arbitrator.

The creation of the mediation-conciliation-compulsory arbitration procedures, to deal with deadlocks, was another important feature of the act These procedures made strikes effectively illegal. The act provided stages for conciliation and mediation by the Commissioner of Labour. As indicated above, the Commissioner of Labour could intervene at any appoint in the dispute, regardless of whether he had been invited or not. If the efforts of the commissioner failed or ended in a deadlock, the matter would be referred for voluntary arbitration if both parties agreed. But where one party to the dispute did not accept voluntary arbitration, the Commissioner of Labour was then statutorily bound under Section 7 of the act to report the dispute to the minister. This section has been amended and the Commissioner will now take the matter to the Industrial Court. Section 9 of the act which empowered the minister to declare an industrial action unlawful has been retained. The minister can still refer a trade dispute to the Industrial Court without the consent of the parties to the dispute. Once the dispute has been referred to the Industrial Court, it is unlawful for workers to continue with the dispute or the industrial action. Before the amendment, Section 20(1) of the act empowered the Permanent Arbitrator, who has now been replaced by the Industrial Court, to make an award to settle a dispute and stipulate that such an award would be binding. The relevant part read:

> Every award of the Permanent Arbitrator shall be binding upon every party to the dispute in question, whether that party did or did not appear or was or was not represented at the hearing and determination of the dispute.

Section 20(2b) of the act stipulated that every award by the Permanent Arbitrator should not be inconsistent with any written law or fail to take into account the *social* and *economic* policies of government. In a situation where a capitalist strategy has been adopted as the state's policy of development, the implication is that the state's social and economic policies will have to ensure that the award of the Permanent Arbitrator should be such that capital will feel protected against any tendencies that might disrupt its accumulation. Whilst Section 20(2b) did not instruct the Permanent Arbitrator on what to do, it remained important as political terms of reference. [12]

Another major area of contention with regard to the Trade Disputes Act is the length it takes to exhaust procedures in order to have a legal strike. Workers have always found themselves in a situation whereby it is impossible to follow all rules and regulations to be able to go on a legal strike. As a result of these cumbersome procedures, Botswana has never had a legal strike since Independence in 1966, and all strikes have been declared illegal in terms of this act. In a survey on trade unions that was conducted for the BFTU (Molutsi et al., 1993) most trade unionists expressed scepticism about the Trade Disputes Act. They pointed out that although the act was formulated to facilitate settlement of disputes, it deliberately makes it impossible to effect legal strikes. In the survey, in which some 151 trade union officials were interviewed, 87 per cent of the respondents felt that in practice it is impossible to have a legal strike and identified the Trade Disputes Act as the source of constraint. Asked which of the labour laws they were most unhappy with, the Trade Disputes Act was the first, followed by the Trade Unions and Emloyers' Organisations Act, with the Employment Act coming last. In the same survey, 72 per cent of the respondents felt that it was not fair for the Commissioner of Labour to intervene in a dispute not reported to him, whilst 65 per cent felt it was not necessary to report a dispute to the Commissioner of Labour unless there was a deadlock. The trade unionists also pointed that the powers of the Commissioner of Labour to intervene in a dispute at any time seriously impeded collective bargaining, or made it virtually irrelevant. Section 4 of the act, which allows the Commissioner of Labour to intervene in disputes not reported to him has been retained.

Industrial action in essential and necessary services

In addition to the constraints mentioned above, industrial action in essential services is curtailed (Section 41 to Section 44 of the Trade Disputes Act), and noncompliance with the tedious procedures automatically renders such industrial action illegal. The procedures for the handling of disputes in essential services are the same as those of handling disputes in general, with the proviso that in essential services, the Commissioner of Labour is given 21 days to resolve the matter, failing which the employees can resort to an industrial action. But the law requires that before such action can commence, there should be a secret ballot supervised by the Commissioner of Labour or his officers. Two thirds majority in favour of an industrial action is required for it to be lawful. However, such industrial action will be illegal if, within the 21 days provided for conciliation and mediation, the minister invokes Section 9 of the act and refers the matter to the Industrial Court, on the grounds that the industrial action would jeopardise the security, the public safety and the essentials of life of the people of Botswana. Industrial action is defined under the Trade Disputes Act as a lockout, strike or action short of a strike in furtherance of a trade dispute. Once the matter has been referred to the Industrial Court, it will be illegal to proceed with an industrial action. The essential services include air traffic control services, the Bank of Botswana, the Botswana Vaccine Institute, electricity and fire services, health and sanitary services, telecommunications, transport and water services, and operation and maintenance of railways. The National Security Act also gives a schedule of necessary services which is identical to those listed as essential services by the Trade Disputes Act. In addition the President of Botswana can declare any other service and facility to be a necessary service. In 1990, the Minister of Labour declared a strike by

91

members of the BBEU unlawful in terms of the Trades Dispute Act and went on to declare banking an essential service. The implications of all these measures for the working class are far reaching. If the minister can declare any service an essential service and the President can also declare any service a necessary service for the purposes of outlawing a strike, what other ways are available for the workers to press for their demands when the only means they have, the industrial action, can be proscribed at the whim of a minister or a head of state?

Labour organisation in the public service

The public sector includes parastatals, the central government and the local government authorities. Public sector workers, except for those working for parastatals, do not fall under the provisions of the Employment Act or any of the country's labour laws. This section of the working class, numbering about 95,000 workers, or more than one third of the formal sector employment, is governed by the Public Service Act. The term "public officer" as it is applied in the context of Botswana is wide and all embracing, and includes everyone from the most junior clerical assistant through to a permanent secretary and the secretary to the cabinet. The definition of a "public officer" is to be inferred from the Constitution of Botswana.

According to Section 127 of the Constitution, a public office means "an office of emoluments in the public service" and the public service means "the civil service of the government", and a "public officer" means "a person holding or acting in any public office". According to the labour laws, a public officer is excluded from the definition of "employee" as defined in the Employment Act. The effect of this exclusion is that all workers in the public sector do not have the right to form and belong to trade unions. They can, by law, belong to staff associations. At the same time there is no collective bargaining in the public service, except for workers in the parastatals. Neither the Public Service Act nor the Constitution of Botswana provides a machinery for the regulation of relations between public sector employees and their employer, the state. However, the act empowers the President to make regulations for the setting up of a body for the purpose of *consultations* between government and public sector workers.

The body that has been created to cater for the interests of the central government public sector workers is the Botswana Civil Servants Association (BCSA), which can only consult, but not enter into collective bargaining. BCSA's method of consultation is as follows. There is a Ministerial Consultative Committee (MCC) for each line ministry. An MCC is chaired by the permanent secretary of that ministry. It is made up of the "staff side", that is the representatives of workers chosen at the annual BCSA conference, and the "management side", that is senior members of the ministry chosen by the permanent secretary.

A regular MCC meeting is devoted to considering submissions from various public officers scattered throughout Botswana, and the issues discussed are on how to make the public service more effective in administering government policy, and not about the welfare of the public officers themselves. Matters of the welfare of an employee in the public sector are between the public officer, his supervisor and the permanent secretary. The permanent secretary may make recommendation to the Director of Public Service Management, or resolve the matter "internally". Some of the issues discussed by the MCC may be resolved by the permanent secretary on the spot, by issuing a directive pronouncing on the matter. Some issues may be taken to the Central Joint Staff Consultative Committee (CJSCC), which is a committee made up of permanent secretaries and some members of the BCSA executive committee. The CJSCC is chaired by the Director of Public Service Management, and the committee may resolve certain issues, or make recommendations to the permanent secretary to the President (who is also the secretary to the cabinet), for him to act on the recommendations or forward them to cabinet.

There are other labour organisations in the public sector, such as the Botswana Unified Local Government Staff Association (BULGASA), the Botswana Federation of Secondary School Teachers (BOFESETE) and the Botswana Primary School Teachers (BOPRITA). None of them can negotiate or enter into collective bargaining with government, and all of them have to channel their views through BCSA which acts as a de facto national centre for public sector labour organisations. The central feature of public sector employment in Botswana is the complete absence of collective bargaining at all levels of the public sector. The public sector employees do not fall under the category of employees in terms of the Employment Act and therefore are not entitled to bargain collectively with their employer. Collective bargaining is defined as a method of negotiation between an employer, a group of employers or one or more employers' organisations on one hand and one or more representatives of the workers' organisations on the other, with a view to reaching an agreement (Farnham and Pimlott, 1992, p. 140). Whilst in developed capitalist countries such as Britain, it has been possible for governments to legislate for the right to belong to trade unions, and to restrict or ban strike actions by workers in certain services such as those that affect national security, law and order and health services, a complete ban on all public sector employees to form and belong to a trade union is unusual.

Botswana and the ILO Conventions

The discussion of Botswana's labour laws and industrial relations system will not be complete without reference to Botswana position regarding the International Labour Organisation (ILO) conventions. Botswana joined the ILO in 1978, immediately after the formation of the BFTU. Though Botswana has been a member since then, the government has not ratified the ILO Conventions essential to the development of free and independent trade unionism. Botswana Government has refused to ratify Convention No. 87/1950, on the freedom of association and protection of the right to organise, Convention No. 98, concerning the application of the principles of the right to organise and bargain collectively, and Convention No. 151 on the protection of the right to organise and the procedures for determining conditions of employment in the public service, commonly known as the Labour Relations (Public Service) Convention (1978). Convention No. 87 states *inter alia*, that "workers and employers ... shall have the right to draw up their constitution and rules, to elect their representatives in full freedom, to organise their administration and activities and to formulate their programmes" and that "public authorities shall refrain from any interference which would restrict this right or impede the lawful exercise thereof". Part II, article 5 of Convention No. 151 on the protection of the right to organise in the public sector states that public employees' organisations shall enjoy complete independence from public authorities, that public employees' organisations shall enjoy adequate protection against any acts of interference by a public authority in their establishment, functioning and administration, and that in particular:

> ... acts which are designed to promote the establishment of public employees' organisations under the domination of a public authority, or to support public employees' organisations by financial or other means, with the object of placing such organisations under the control of a public authority, shall be deemed to constitute acts of interference within the meaning of this article.

However as of January 1994, Botswana had ratified only two ILO Conventions, all dating back to the 1920s. These are Convention No. 14/1921, on weekly rest (industry) and Convention No. 19/925, on equality of treatment (accident compensation). [13]

A question may be posed as to what the relevance of the ILO Conventions is to the analysis of labour law in Botswana, especially because where international conventions are at variance with laws of a sovereign country, national laws prevail. This question is important for three reasons. Firstly, as a member of the ILO, Botswana is expected, though by no means required, to abide by these conventions, otherwise there is very little sense in belonging to such an organisation. Secondly, ratification of these laws will mean that Botswana has to put them into effect, and this would mean removing Section 13(2) of the Constitution, which, as I have pointed out, was enacted specifically to control the labour movement in both the private sector and in the public sector. Lastly, ratification will subject Botswana to the ILO supervisory machinery.

Conclusion

This chapter has mapped out the legal environment and has revealed the various forms of labour control embodied in the labour legislation. These forms of control involve a variety of strategies such as the state's creation of minimum conditions

94

of service and protection of basic rights, as provided for in the Employment Act, the intervention of the state, through the Labour Office, in industrial disputes, to mediate, conciliate and if necessary order compulsory arbitration to break any bargaining deadlock, the denial of the state employees the right to form and belong to trade unions and the creation of an alternative and less demanding form of representation in the public sector. The last two ones have had the effect of limiting the strength of organised labour in the public service by emasculating its capacity to bargain collectively with the employer. The restrictions on the trade union rights and freedoms in Botswana provide a typical example of the shortcomings that are characteristic of bourgeois democracy. As Marx and Engels (1968) argued, these freedoms are only dressed in "a constitutional uniform". Each of these freedoms is proclaimed as the absolute right of the citizen, but always with the "marginal" note that it is unlimited so far as it is not limited by other laws. As Marx pointed out:

> [Each] paragraph of the Constitution contains its own antithesis, its own upper house and lower house, namely, freedom in the general phrase, abrogation of freedom in the marginal note. Thus so long as the *name* of freedom was respected and only its actual realisation prevented, of course in a legal way, the constitutional existence of freedom remained intact, inviolate, however mortal the blows dealt to its existence *in actual life* (1968a, pp. 107-8).

Although the state has not sought to impose a constitution on either the BFTU or the national unions, or to impose a secretary general as it happened in Kenya or in Ghana, nonetheless the state still defines the parameters of the organisation of the trade union movement both internally and externally. The legal environment within which the trade union movement has been operating in the last three decades has seriously constrained its development and limited its autonomy. It constitutes a system of labour repression. Thus Hyman (1975) is vindicated when he argues that an industrial relations system is just an element in the totality of capitalist relations of production: it does not presuppose consensus, but it is a relation of domination and subordination. It is a process of control over work relations in which job regulation is merely one of the many forms of such control.

But having said all this, it must be pointed out that there have been changes in the political economy of Botswana. These changes have been accompanied by quantitative and qualitative changes in the composition of the working class and the awakening consciousness on the part of the workers. Whilst the state's industrial relations practices such as the wages policy and labour laws have provided objective structural limitations within which the working class could perceive their options, the working class has gradually developed their own counter ideologies and counter discourses and learnt, in the course of the ongoing confrontation with the state and the capital, that it can challenge the system. Neither the state nor the capital have a monopoly of political or ideological dominance. As Marx (1968a, pp. 37-8) argued, one of the progressive roles played by capitalism is that wherever

95

it had got the upper hand, it had put to an end all social relations that bound people to their "natural superiors", and had left remaining "no other nexus between man and man than naked self interest". It is this self interest that propels workers forward. As Hyman (1975, p. 6) argues, the social contradiction which offers the greatest potential for structural change is that between the independent collective character of the productive activity and the concentration of ownership and control of economic resources in a small number of hands. According to Hyman, the spontaneous collaboration which modern production requires, offers a basis for collective intervention of workers to transform society, and the crucial additional ingredient for such a transformation is a conscious organisation in pursuit of this objective. Botswana workers have at times displayed a capacity to resist their domination by the state and the capital. These acts sought to exert the autonomy of labour and challenge the hegemony of capital albeit within the limits of the structures of state control, domination and subordination. This is discussed in the next chapter.

Notes

1   *The Botswana Daily News,* 8 June 1969.

2   *The Botswana Daily News*, 18 June 1969.

3   Ibid.

4   Ibid.

5   Section 7 of the act empowers the minister to restrict application of the act, and the government has restricted the application of the act in the case of domestic workers, i.e. workers employed in small undertakings such as cattle posts or doing household work for a family.

6   Interview with Ronald Baipidi, former secretary general of the BFTU, 27 August 1991.

7   Ibid.

8   Minister Kwelagobe's address to the BFTU Delegates Conference, 23 June 1984.

9   Ibid.

10   Peter Olsen, a Gaborone based labour consultant and managing director of Tsa Badiri, Labour and Management Consultants.

11   Interview with Isaac Mabiletsa, former executive committee member (BFTU), now a Member of Parliament for BNF, 30 August 1991.

12   The Permanent Arbitrator was a person qualified to be appointed as a judge of the High Court of Botswana, with the same privileges, immunities and protection. The Permanent Arbitrator was Mr O.M.Mapitse - an Assistant Attorney General. The act establishing the Industrial Court stipulates that Industrial Court judges shall be persons possessing the qualifications to be a puisne judge.

13   International Labour Organisation (1995), *List of Ratifications by Convention and by Country*: Geneva.

7 Trade union growth and development

Introduction

One of the key features in the development of capitalism and capitalist relations of production is the growth of formal sector employment, whereby the labour force is freed from the traditional non-wage economic activities, such as subsistence agricultural production, into wage labour. The economic growth policies of the postcolonial era have led to a significant structural transformation in various sectors of the economy. These have led to growth in formal sector employment and have rapidly expanded the social base of the working class on an ever increasing scale. The process of industrialisation, the separation of direct producers from their means of production, and their reconstitution as a "proletariat" increases the potential for workers to constitute themselves in a new class organisation, the trade union. It is the trade union that accentuates the class struggle against capitalism. This latter point is discussed fully in the next chapter. The purpose of this chapter is to give an overview of the growth and development of the trade union movement in Botswana. Trade unions, and the movement of class of which they are a part, are dynamic social organisations that develop both quantitatively and qualitatively over time. Working class consciousness is also a dynamic phenomenon. With time, trade unions gain experience, confidence and foresight in their dealings with the state and the capital.

The state of the trade unions

In Botswana, as in the rest of sub-Saharan Africa, the development of trade unionism to a large extent parallels the late arrival of capitalism in this part of the world. Until the 1940s there were no trade unions in the country. The persistent underdevelopment of the economy and the absence of wage labour on any significant scale ensured that there was virtually no working class to support a trade union movement. The opportunities for formal employment were in South Africa, where most of Botswana's workers went as migrant workers. Because of the limited extent of industrialisation during the colonial period, the first trade unions in Botswana, as in many other parts of Africa, were concentrated in the lower and middle ranks of the civil service and public enterprises such as the Public Works Department (PWD) (Gladstone, 1980).

The first trade union in Botswana was the whites only European Civil Service Association, formed in 1948. It was followed by the formation of the African Civil Service Association in 1949. These two existed as parallel organisations, speaking on behalf of white and black employees respectively. After Independence, the two merged to form BCSA - the civil servants association. In the very small private sector side, the first trade union to appear was the FAEU, which was formed in 1949. The FAEU was a local union based in Francistown, in the north-east of Botswana. The FAEU was open to all workers in all manner of employment, except to public officers. Most of its membership were unskilled and semiskilled labourers with very little formal education (Simkin, 1975). According to Simkin, the FAEU collapsed about six years after its formation due to such problems as poor quality leadership, lack of resources and financial mismanagement.

The first attempts to form a countrywide trade union were made in 1959 with the formation of the BPWU. The BPWU had its headquarters in Serowe, and branches in Mahalapye in central Botswana, Lobatse in the south and Maun in the north. In 1963, the BTUC (a trade unions congress) was established and was later instrumental in the formation of the BGWO (the general workers' organisation) in 1964 (Motshidisi, 1975). However, the trade union movement really took off only in the 1970s, when a number of collective labour agreements with various employers were concluded. The first collective labour agreement was signed in March 1972 between the BCGWU (the commercial and general workers' union) and the Botswana Breweries Ltd. The BMWU entered its first collective labour agreement with the mining house, Bamangwato Concessions Ltd (BCL) in 1972, and later with De Beers Mining (1973). The BBEU (the bank union) concluded its first collective labour agreement in 1974, with Barclays and Standard Chartered - the only two commercial banks in Botswana at that time. These collective labour agreements were not just symbolic or formal, but were indicative of the growing awareness on the part of the trade unions in Botswana. They opened the way for more collective agreements by other unions and strengthened unionism in Botswana.

The increase in formal employment has meant that, at least theoretically, more workers have come into the labour market to support trade unions. Table 7.1 shows the key sectors in terms of employment, and also the trend in employment patterns. By March 1995, formal sector employment in all sectors stood at 234,500. It is estimated that about 10,000 of the employees were noncitizens. According to the table, the private sector has emerged as the largest employer. The table shows that in March 1995, private sector employment stood at 136,500, or about 56 per cent of total employment, and the public sector had a total of 98,000 workers or 42 per

Table 7.1

Estimated number of paid employees by sector and economic activity, 1986-95 (selected years)

Sector/ Economic activity	August 1981	September 1985	March 1991	March 1993	March 1995
Agriculture	4,800	400	6,700	5,900	4,700
Mining and quarrying	2,300	7,300	7,800	8,400	8,400
Manufacturing	6,400	9,100	26,000	22,100	23,400
Electricity and water	1,600	1,200	2,500	2,600	2,600
Construction	15,200	19,500	33,800	28,300	22,600
Commerce	15,300	18,300	41,000	40,700	47,100
Transport and communication	3,900	5,700	9,100	9,800	9,300
Finance and business services	4,900	6,800	16,100	16,800	18,300
Community and personal services	3,800	3,900	8,600	8,200	10,000
Education	1,600	1,900	2,500	2,600	3,100
Subtotal Private	-	-	142,500	131,800	136,500
Parastatals	-	-	11,800	13,700	13,100
Private and parastatals	64,800	71,200	154,300	145,500	149,600
Cental government	32,600	45,600	55,500	65,800	69,400
Local government	-	-	13,000	14,900	15,600
Total all sectors	97,400	116,800	222,800	226,200	234,500

Source: Ministry of Finance and Development Planning (1996), *Annual Economic Report.*

cent of total employment. The public sector was made up of the central government, with employment level of 69,400, local government with 15,600 and the parastatals with 13,100. The five dominant sectors in terms of employment were: commerce - 47,000, construction - 22,600, manufacturing - 23,400 and finance and business services with 18,300. With 42 per cent of total employment, the state remains the largest single employer. That commerce should account for 47,000 workers or about 35 per cent of total private sector employment says a lot about the nature of Botswana capitalist development. It is a dependent form of capitalism which is more about distribution than about production or manufacturing. The manufacturing sector accounts for only 17 per cent of total private sector employment.

Table 7.2 shows registered trade unions affiliated to the BFTU. There are in all more than 20 trade unions in Botswana, and only a handful are not affiliated to the BFTU. The BFTU remains the only federation of trade unions. As the table indicates, these trade unions are organised along industrial lines to conform to the 1968 Trade Unions Act, and they cover the whole spectrum of the economy. By January 1996, total trade union membership stood at 66,886. Based on the current private sector employment figure of 136,500 (Table 7.1), plus the 40,000 industrial class employees in the public sector, trade union density stands at about 38 per cent. It is possible that trade union membership and trade union density could be higher if the public sector workers were not denied the right to form and belong to trade unions. But compared with some developed capitalist countries where there has been a decline in trade union membership, this is not a bad performance. In 1988 trade union density was highest in Sweden at 85.3 per cent, and lowest in France at 12 per cent. In Britain trade union density stood at 41.5 per cent in the same year.[1]

By far the largest union in Botswana is the Manual Workers' Union. In January 1996 the estimated membership of this union stood at 40,000. The Manual Workers' Union is an organisation of the so called industrial class employees in the public sector, that is in central government, local authorities and parastatals. The union therefore represents the blue collar section of the state workers. The white collar public sector employees belong to BCSA - an "association" registered in terms of the Societies Act, rather than the Trade Unions and Employers' Organisations Act. Next in line in terms of membership strength is the BCGWU, with a membership of 8,890. The BCGWU, it will be recalled from Chapter 6, is the only general union. It was exempted from the restructuring process of the late 1960s. The next in line is the construction workers' union (the BCWU) with a membership of 8,234, followed by the BMWU (the mine workers' union) with an estimated membership of 3,401, followed by the BMIWU (the meat workers' union) with a membership of 1,665, and the BRWU (the railway workers' union) with 1,125. The rest of the unions are very small, with a membership of less than a thousand. However, these small trade unions include the BBEU (the bank union), which, despite its size, is one of Botswana's best organised, well resourced and militant unions.

101

Table 7.2
Registered trade unions and estimated membership (January 1996)

	Name of union	Headquarters	Estimated membership
1	Manual Workers' Union	Gaborone	40,000
2	Commercial and General Workers' Union	Gaborone	8,890
3	Construction Workers' Union	Gaborone	8,234
4	Mine Workers' Union	Selebi-Phikwe	5,441
5	Railway Workers' Union	Gaborone	605
6	Meat Workers' Union	Lobatse	560
7	Telecommunications Employees' Union	Gaborone	544
8	Bank Employees' Union	Gaborone	400
9	Power Corporation Workers' Union	Palapye	400
10	Beverages and Allied Workers' Union	Gaborone	300
11	Postal Services Workers' Union	Gaborone	322
12	Housing Corporation Staff Union	Gaborone	336
13	Diamond Sorters and Valuators' Union	Gaborone	260
14	Central Bank Union	Gaborone	150
15	Railway Senior Staff Union	Mahalapye	157
16	Railway Staff and Artisan Employees' Union	Gaborone	126
17	National Development Bank Staff Union	Gaborone	85
18	Agricultural Marketing Board Workers' Union	Gaborone	46
19	Vaccine Institute Staff Union	Gaborone	30
		Total	*66,886*

Source: Registrar of Trade Unions and Employers' Organisations; Botswana Federation of Trade Unions; National Unions.

Sectionalism and class consciousness

As pointed out above, it was capitalism that brought about the working class in the first instance. As result trade unions have not only emerged as a part of the capitalist economy, but they have also been organised according to the capitalist division of labour. The sectional character of trade unions therefore derives from the sectional character of capitalism. Because trade unions are organised along sectional lines rather than class lines, there is a tendency for some sections of the trade union movement to focus on the short term interests of particular groups of workers rather than the long term class interests (Kelly, 1988, pp. 54-7). This has led to a problem of sectionalism in the working class movement. Sectionalism can be defined as a working class consciousness in which one's own group interests are placed above those of the other groups either within a trade union or across trade unions. According to Kelly, one important litmus test for the growth of class consciousness is whether trade unions are able to transcend the problem of sectionalism and develop a corporate consciousness, that is, identify their sectional interests with those of a large corporate body, such as a national federation, and thus with the working class as a whole. Working class consciousness can also by judged by the transition from corporate consciousness to more hegemonic interests, that is, when the working class as a whole identifies their interests with those of the society as a whole (Kelly, 1988, p. 88).

The trade union movement in Botswana has not escaped the problem of sectionalism. One problem concerns national unions relationship to the BFTU. One official of the BFTU executive has confirmed in an interview that some BFTU affiliates have not been giving the BFTU secretariat correct information about their membership because they want to avoid paying increased subscription to the BFTU. Subscription to the BFTU is based on the level of membership. According to the interviewee, some national unions have developed a tendency of giving the lowest figure in order to pay the lowest subscription. In fact a study of the files on trade unions annual returns at the office of the Registrar of Trade Unions and Employers' Organisations gives the impression that trade unions have not had any increase in their membership for several years. This was surprising considering the fact that employment in Botswana has been on the increase for several years. The interviewee opined that:

> Workers have not yet been conscientised. They do see the value of belonging to trade unions. At the same time some workers have been threatened by employers that they would be sacked if they belong to trade unions. This is against the law. But when we try to investigate, workers do not come out because they fear victimisation. There is very little that we can do as BFTU to fight this anti-trade union activity.[2]

Other problems identified by the informant concern (a) the generation gap, (b) gender, and (c) commitment and support for one's trade union. On the problem of the generation gap, Baipidi pointed out that this has manifested itself when it comes to adopting resolution for industrial actions. He said that older members were very conservative and had been a constraining factor on the younger ones who were more militant because they were aware that they were still marketable, and could go and look for another job. According to Baipidi, when a union wants to call for a strike actions, the older members are reluctant, saying that they have to think about their families first. On the problem of gender, it was pointed out that some male members in some unions are opposed to paid maternity leave, saying that they are being overworked. "They say that it is unfair for women to go on maternity leave on full pay, when they [male workers] are the ones who are being overworked as a result of the women employees' absence". As my informant pointed out, some male workers are just jealous of the advantages that females get over them. On the problem of commitment to trade unionism, Baipidi singled out the white collar workers as the least dedicated. He pointed out that when the BFTU proposed that subscription to the national unions should be a check off system, based on a percentage of one's salary it was the white collar workers who resisted, arguing that they will be paying more for identical services. At the same time, the white collar workers think they have everything, and remember about the union only when they are fired. "The lower income group are the keen unionists" he pointed out. He continued:

> The white collar workers are the least dedicated, if their attendance of our meetings is anything to go by. But look at the manual workers. They are the most militant and disciplined, and they support their union all the way. These are the most exploited workers. If the leadership calls for a strike action, they never hesitate. They have nothing to loose. They do not start thinking about housing and car loans when they have to take industrial action. They do not start worrying about where they will get the money to pay their instalments if they are fired. They have no loans with the company or the banks.[3]

The problems of the labour movement in Botswana, some of which have been described by the secretary general can be better characterised by the concept of "interior determination". This involves the transmission of some elements of the bourgeois culture (including bourgeois individualism) which become accepted or even generated by the institutions of proletarian culture itself (Cohen and Henderson, 1991). For example, the negative attitude or lack of enthusiasm displayed by the white collar workers towards the trade union movement reveals how much they have internalised white collar mentality. They believe that because they are white collar workers and have relatively good salaries and mortgages and car loans, they have everything they want. They are inclined to support the status quo, or at the very least, not to rock the boat. Thus to the list of strategies of control such as bonus schemes, pensions, gratuities, and promotions benefits such as company or bank loans can be added. It would seem that these strategies have met with some measure of success, insofar as they have separated white collar workers from their blue collar colleagues. As we can see in the remarks made by the secretary general, solidarity between the white collar workers and blue collar workers is very low. The point to bear in mind about this particular problem of sectionalism of the white collar workers is a result of the capitalist division of the labour process into white collar and blue collar. This is also a consequence of the degradation and fragmentation of the labour process under capitalism, into the such categories as "unskilled", "semiskilled", "skilled" and "expert" workers. This degradation and fragmentation of the labour process created a privileged stratum or a "labour aristocracy" which has developed a work orientation that subjectively puts it on the side of capital, although objectively it remains part of the working class. This explains why white collar workers do not remember their trade unions except when they are in trouble. This mentality has also been reinforced by another strategy of labour control, the creation of the so called "staff unions" as a separate entity from the "regular" trade union of the "rank and file" workers. This sectionalism has actually been buttressed by the law. The pity of it all is that this form of habituation is accepted and transmitted through proletarian culture and institutions (Cohen and Henderson, 1991).

Collective bargaining

One of the most striking features of Botswana's industrial relations system is the weakness of organised labour vis-à-vis capital in the process of collective bargaining and negotiations on various labour issues, including the settlement of labour disputes. This fact was acknowledged by the former Commissioner of Labour when he pointed out that:

> While the labour movement and the Labour Department constitute a weaker and a weak partner respectively in the tripartite structure of our national labour relations machinery, the employer constitutes a strong partner. His representation is often by a mature and experienced personnel officer. In urban areas of Gaborone, Francistown, Selebi Phikwe, Lobatse, Orapa and Jwaneng, the employer's representative is often a retired top public officer, i.e. an ex-permanent secretary, a lawyer or a representative of a consultancy company.[4]

While it is true that the BFTU cannot afford to employ a top labour lawyer or a labour economist, or a host of other experts that are found at BOCCIM, there are two other important constraints not mentioned by the Labour Commissioner, namely (a) lack of disclosure of information for collective bargaining, and (b) absence of formal structures for collective bargaining. It is doubtful even in the event the BFTU could raise enough cash to hire experts to assist them in any collective bargaining, especially in wage and salary determination, that these people could do their work effectively. The Trade Unions and Employers' Organisations

Act stipulates that once a trade union has been registered, the employer is expected in terms of Section 50(1) to deal with the trade union as the negotiating body in respect of all matters of employment. However, neither the Trade Unions and Employers' Organisations Act nor the Trade Disputes Act (as amended), make any provisions for the disclosure of information for the purpose of collective bargaining. In other words, although legally an employer is compelled to recognise a registered trade union and deal with it in collective bargaining negotiations, the employer is not under any legal obligation to disclose to the workers' side financial and other information concerning the company's performance. This is yet another strategy of labour control because it impedes the ability of trade unions to bargain effectively. Salamon (1987, p. 245) defines disclosure of information for collective bargaining as:

> [The] transfer to employee representatives of information generated as an integral part of the managerial function of planning, controlling and decision making and traditionally retained within the exclusive possession of management.

In Botswana, employers have no legal duty to keep their employees informed about the state of the enterprise. Most trade unionists have argued that they usually go to the negotiating table with no factual information or knowledge that they can use to conduct meaningful collective bargaining (Molutsi et al., 1993). The question that arises is, what really is the significance of automatic recognition of trade unions and the legal requirement that employers should negotiate with registered trade unions in their industries, when the management is under no obligation to give out information for that purpose? This is another situation where the state gives with one hand and takes with the other.

Admittedly, the disclosure of information for the purpose of collective bargaining is a controversial and sensitive issue. Salamon (1987, pp. 247-8) argues that managers have always resisted the disclosure of information for various reasons. One reason that has been put forward by the managers is that in the competitive and conflictual environment of collective bargaining, the possession of knowledge by one party to the exclusion of the other is an important determinant of relative power and that any disclosure of such exclusive knowledge may affect the balance of power to the detriment of the management. Another reason given is that the disclosure of managerial information on a formal and regular basis may lead to pressure for the expansion of joint regulation into much wider areas of decision making, because the assumptions, logic and implications of such information may be questioned or debated by the recipients. The other reason which Salamon cites is that managers are reluctant to disclose information because it may be imprecise and thus reflect adversely on their capability and credibility to manage. In the developed capitalist countries like Britain, there exists a legal requirement for the disclosure of information for the purpose of collective bargaining. The question that remains is, what type of information must be disclosed.

According to Salamon, in Britain there exists a requirement to release to the workers' side information without which the trade union negotiators will be to a material extent impeded in carrying on collective bargaining. For instance, the Advisory, Conciliation and Arbitration Services (ACAS) Code of Practice provides guidance to the range of information which management may be expected to disclose for the purpose of collective bargaining. It includes information concerning the performance of the company, that is, data on productivity and efficiency, savings from increased productivity and output, return on capital invested and sales, and data about the state of the order book. Companies may also be required to disclose financial information, that is, cost structures, gross and net profits, allocation of profits, sources of earnings, assets and liabilities, details of government financial assistance, transfer prices, loans to parent or subsidiary companies and interest charged (Salamon, 1987, pp. 249-50).

However, this development must be seen in the proper context, which is that in developed liberal capitalist countries there has been a general pressure within the society for more openness in political and governmental systems at all levels. The pressure on commerce and industry is therefore directly linked to these societal pressures. However in small peripheral countries like Botswana, with their industrialisation dependent on foreign investment, it is not easy to make such demands on foreign investors, with the pressure that international capitalism can exert on the peripheral state. In its quest for foreign investment, the peripheral state in turn exerts pressure and incapacitates the labour movement in various ways. Lack of disclosure of information is therefore one of the several mechanisms used to paralyse the trade union movement. This is the first handicap for union negotiators in Botswana.

The second handicap concerns the absence of proper structures for collective bargaining. Although trade unions are compelled by law to organise along industrial lines, capital has been allowed to remain amorphous, with no corresponding employers' organisations. One trade unionist pointed out that trade unions are made deliberately weak by being forced to negotiate at plant or enterprise level. He argued that the present employer's organisation, BOCCIM, is just a heterogeneous organisation of various employers:

> BOCCIM cannot address the regulation of the relationship between employers and employees. [At BOCCIM] they are more concerned about profit. BOCCIM cannot have a role in industrial relations because it is not an industrial organisation. Trade unions in Botswana have been formed along industrial lines, but they have no counterpart employers' organisations to negotiate with. What workers want is employers' organisations to negotiate with, not to negotiate with the management of a particular plant or enterprise.[5]

These views were echoed by the national organising secretary of the Manual Workers' Union, who pointed out that the only collective agreement that exists is between the government and the union, and this only affects workers in central government. There is no collective agreement with either local authorities or public corporations. He argued:

> The biggest problem facing our union is that although the union has been registered as one union in accordance with the Trade Unions and Employers' Organisations Act, we have three different employers. These employers have different powers and resources. We therefore have to negotiate separate agreements for the members of one union. This presents obvious difficulties. Some members may feel that they are not adequately represented when their colleagues in other sectors gain better conditions or wages, or that they are left behind. They do not understand that these employers have different resources. It is even difficult for industrial workers in local authorities to understand how they cannot have the same conditions of service as their counterparts in central government. But we are negotiating with our three employers so that we can have common industrial class regulations to cover all manual workers throughout the country. We want one consultative machinery in which employers' representatives will face workers' representatives. At the moment industrial workers in local authorities are not covered by the unified local government regulations. Each local authority controls its employees in its own way. We are proposing a joint consultative machinery that will comprise council secretaries and town clerks on one hand and ourselves on the other.[6]

Now to return to the question of human resources. The Commissioner of Labour alluded to the fact that one of the weaknesses of the labour movement is that it does not have the calibre of manpower that the employers have. However this is related to the fact the Trade Unions and Employers' Organisations Act plays a part in weakening the trade unions and thus strengthening the hand of capital. The managers of capital have a habit of depriving the trade unions of their most educated and experienced leaders who have no sooner been elected into trade union office than the employer "kicks them upstairs" into "pseudomanagerial" positions.[7] Once workers have been promoted into managerial positions, they lose their trade union membership rights, as they are now members of the management. Section 61(12)(c) of the Trade Unions and Employers' Organisations Act defines a member of the management as:

> ... an employee who is employed in a capacity that requires him to have full knowledge of the financial position of the undertaking or enterprise in which he is employed or gives him personal access to other confidential information relating to the conduct of his employer's business.

The tactic of the managers of capital to "promote" educated and experienced trade unionists in order to silence them and at the same time weaken the trade union has become a very popular management weapon against trade unions. Employees who have thus been promoted are not expected to have anything to do with a trade union but may join a "staff" union. At the centre of the "bogus promotion" is the question whether an employee has the right not to accept promotion, especially if that promotion is viewed with suspicion by the employee or the union.

Although this tactic is alleged to have been used over the years, the first test case was only brought to court in 1990 in the case of Tamasiga versus National Development Bank.[8] The details of the case are that the applicant was a senior projects officer at the bank head office and the chairman of the staff union. Tamasiga was suddenly transferred to another post in Serowe, some 300 km north-west of Gaborone. He refused to go on transfer, and after some time his contract with the bank was terminated by the bank. The applicant appealed to the Labour Office, citing Section 27 of the Employment Act, which gives the employee the right to protest against termination of contract of employment. The Labour Officer confirmed the transfer and the subsequent termination, but ordered that Tamasiga be awarded compensation equal to two months basic salary.

Tamasiga then applied to the High Court for reinstatement. In his submission Tamasiga based his application for reinstatement first on the law of contract. He asked the court to rule in his favour on the grounds that the transfer was an unreasonable instruction as the position of assistant regional manager did not exist and that this put him at risk. He further argued that the transfer amounted to a demotion because whereas his present position entitled him to approve projects of up to P20,000, the position of assistant regional manager limited him to projects of up to P10,000. He further argued that his academic qualifications, a BA degree in economics and statistics and a MBA, were those of a projects officer and not of a regional manager, and that the position of a projects officer is different in content, rank and status from that of an assistant regional manager. Secondly, the applicant sought reinstatement because he believed that the transfer was a victimisation for his trade union activities, that is to say, the management wished to curtail or hamper his trade union activity by sending him to an isolated place and promoting him to the post of assistant regional manager. The applicant invoked Section 23 of the Employment Act, which prohibited employers to terminate employment on the grounds of trade union membership. Tamasiga also told the court that he has told his employer that he did not want to become an assistant regional manager and that he had decided not to accept the offer.[9]

In his ruling the judge said that there was no way that a letter of transfer could be construed as an offer that the applicant was entitled to accept or refuse. The judge referred to one of the bank's condition of service which said that "an employee shall be liable to serve in any branch of the bank within Botswana and to perform the bank's business anywhere outside Botswana". In his concluding remarks, the judge pointed out:

> I have therefore come to the conclusion that there was an order of transfer and that order was lawful and not made with an ulterior motive of preventing the applicant rendering service to the union. In any event, I pause here to point

out that his salary was paid by the bank. His first duty in terms of his employment was to the bank and if he felt that he could not render service to both the bank and the union then in my view he had to make a choice.[10]

While this on the surface seems a straight forward judicial pronouncement based on a sound and diligent interpretation of a contract of employment, critical analysis reveals the inequality embodied in the contract of employment under capitalist relations of production. In this relationship, the worker does not only surrender his capacity to work to the employer, but even cedes his right to accept or refuse redeployment. As Crouch (1977, pp. 4-5) points out:

> At the core of both class relations and industrial relations is the economic relationship of domination and subordination: the labour contract. In exchange for his wages the worker places his labour at the disposal of the employer. This relationship is distinguished from other commercial contracts in that the worker accepts a role of subordination ... For a specific wage payment the employer acquires a generalised capacity to control the labour ... It may well be the case that within the terms of the relationship subordinates are occasionally able to exercise more situational "power"; but this should not obscure the fact that the employment relationship is necessarily one in which one party places itself under the control of the other.

The judgement in Tamasiga versus National Development Bank is an example of how the principle of the rule of law conceals the fact that the applicant's interests are subordinate to that of the employer. This inequality enables the law to resolve a dispute by virtue of its power rather than its impartiality (Fine, 1984).

Settlement of labour disputes

The Trade Disputes Act was amended in June 1992, to pave the way for the establishment of the Industrial Court. All labour disputes must first be lodged with the Commissioner of Labour for conciliation and mediation. If during this process the Commissioner of Labour forms the view that he cannot help in the matter, he can in accordance with Section 7 of the Trade Disputes Act (as amended) issue a certificate allowing the disputants to take the matter to the Industrial Court. The Industrial Court is not the final court, so the disputants can pursue the matter up to the Court of Appeal. According to Lebang and Olsen (1990), by 1989, that is before the creation of the Industrial Court, district labour offices around the country had recorded some 5,478 individual grievances, with 4,636 carried over from the previous years. By 1990 some 5,803 cases were still pending. Most disputes concerned breaches of statutory provisions of the Employment Act and the Trade Disputes Act. These figures give an indication of the load of cases that the Commissioner of Labour and the district labour offices have to deal with. But the other important thing is that workers are beginning to be more conscious of their rights and are prepared to fight for them. The mere awareness of the existence of these rights is a positive development in the consciousness of the workers.

Between April 1994 and July 1996, the Industrial Court registered about 300 disputes. However only ten per cent of the disputes were collective labour disputes, brought by trade unions or in some cases by a group of nonunionised workers. Most of the these were about rights involving the interpretation of individual labour law such as unfair or unlawful dismissals. In other words, even collective disputes were over rights, as opposed to disputes over the economic or political interests of the trade unions. For example, there was a case of dispute over rights which involved a nonunionised group of *Batswana* artisans. The artisans complained to the Commissioner of Labour that their salaries were 40 per cent lower than those of expatriate artisans from South Africa, who happened to have the same qualifications and experience as *Batswana* artisans, and that these pay differentials were discriminatory and contravened the Employment Act. The management defended themselves by arguing that the 40 per cent differential was made up of allowances that government accepts as inducement for expatriates. However, because the basic salaries and the "allowances" were in a package, the arbitrator refused to accept the management argument and ordered that local artisans must be paid the same amount as their expatriate counterparts. But because this was a voluntary arbitration, the management appealed to the High Court. The court found that the minister was wrong in ordering arbitration, and declared it null and void.[11]

The case of a collective dispute that involved a dispute of economic interests of the workers was that of *Mine Workers' Union versus BCL Mining Company*. The facts of the case are that the union proposed to management a 40 per cent wage and salary increase across the board for certain grades. The management countered by saying that they wanted to negotiate the introduction of economic rents and the phasing out of subsidies to the workers. The union wanted the two issues to be discussed separately. This resulted in a deadlock and the matter was referred to voluntary arbitration. The Permanent Arbitrator agreed with the union that the two issues should be negotiated separately, and awarded the union a 30 per cent wage increase as against their proposed 40 per cent, but nevertheless substantially higher than the 10 per cent suggested by the management. Of particular interest are the reasons for this award. The arbitrator pointed out in his judgement that the union has a good case because in the first place, workers work a longer week than workers in the public sector whose wages and salaries have been raised by 10 per cent recently. The arbitrator rejected the management's argument that the company would not be able to sustain the pay increase because the prices of metals were volatile. He said that the 10 per cent salary increase in the public sector was a cost of living award and not a wage and salary increase. He said that the BCL had not been profitable for a number of years and had been unable to meet its liabilities. However, there were now indications that the situation had changed as the company had started paying its creditors and that the award "takes into account the sacrifices made by the employees of BCL during the lean years that the BCL went through". The Permanent Arbitrator observed:

> The history of the union in this dispute of wage increase has shown remarkable appreciation of the circumstances under which BCL has been operating its mine. It has shown restraint in not asking for wage increases during the difficult periods during which the mine operated. It is only proper that when the company is making an operating profit that recognition be given to the fact that inflation has eroded whatever purchasing power the employees had, more so given their forbearance in making up for that loss of purchasing power. It is therefore unreasonable on the part of management to keep on insisting that the bad times are not over, when in the current two years of the history of the mine profits were made and legal liabilities were being met, to ask the union to forego a modest increase.[12]

A more recent case of disputes over the economic rights of the workers was the case of *Debswana Diamond Company versus Mine Workers' Union*. The management and the union failed to reach agreement and the matter was referred to the Industrial Court. During wage negotiations the union demanded an 18 per cent wage increase across the board against the management offer of two per cent across the board and one per cent service award. The union also demanded that maternity leave should be raised to 85 per cent from 65 per cent, and a shift allowance be increased from 10 per cent to 18 per cent. The workers cited increased profitability of the company as the ground for their wages demand. The Industrial Court ruled that employees could not expect a share in the profits of the company unless there was a share agreement which would include sharing the losses just like any other shareholder. The court further ruled that employers had no legal or moral duty to increase wages to keep pace with inflation; that affordability was not a relevant factor; that there was no entitlement to an increase; and that the demand for wages could not be measured in terms of level of profit.[13]

Conclusion

The economic structure of postcolonial Botswana has made possible the development of a working class. The pre-Independence Botswana was in the main characterised by both undeveloped capitalist productive forces and uneven development of capitalist relations of production within the country itself. The working class was just too small and organisationally weak to conduct any significant class struggle in a social formation whose relations of production were predominantly noncapitalist. This kind of economic structure placed limitations on the development of the working class and class struggle in the country. The strength of trade unions derive from the extent of the spread of capitalist relations, that is, in tandem with the development of capitalism. Although trade unions in

Botswana are committed to working within the capitalist system, they have nevertheless striven to fight for the interests of the workers even within the limits of that system. This is much demonstrated in the legal actions that trade unions have taken against employers. It can be argued that the trade union movement has at least fulfilled two important functions of the trade union movement, namely providing elementary resistance and defending the immediate economic interests of its members. Trade unions work well as far as they counteract, even if temporarily, the tendency to a fall in the general rate of wages. Their great merit in their struggle to keep up wages is that they tend to keep up and to raise the standard of living of members (Draper, 1978, pp. 94-5) Insofar as trade unions can use their organisations to defend their immediate legal, social, and economic interests, to fight the effects of exploitation and to retard the downward movement in their standard of living, alleviating the miseries that capitalism imposes on them, then they are at least fulfilling the minimum expectations of the role of a trade union. As Marx pointed out (Draper, 1978), trade union struggles are an indispensable means of holding up the spirit of the labouring masses, to prevent them from becoming apathetic, thoughtless, and more or less well fed instruments of production. Trade unions still remain the real organisation of the workers in which they carry out their daily struggles with capital (Draper, 1978).

The workers are now organised in organisations, and they are beginning to carry out their demands as organisations. This is by no means a sufficient condition for class struggle, but it is a necessary one. As Marx (Marx and Engels, 1953) pointed out, trade union struggles are class struggle because in the course of confrontation with capital, the workers become united in their trade unions, and the interests they defend become class interests, and the struggle of class against class is a political struggle.

Notes

1   International Labour Organisation (1992), *World Labour Report*, p. 156.
2   Interview with Ronald Baipidi, former secretary general of the BFTU, 27 August 1991.
3   Ibid.
4   *Department of Labour Annual Report* (1989), p. 33.
5   Interview with Martin Setlhare, former administrative secretary of the BMWU, 14 November 1991.
6   Interview with Johnson Motshwarakgole, National Organising Secretary of the Manual Workers' Union, 4 November 1991.
7   Ibid.
8   Ibid.
9   Civil Case No. 116/91, 15 September 1992.
10   Ibid.

11   Judgement on *Local Artisans (Jwaneng Mine) versus Debswana Diamond Company*, Jwaneng, 28 December 1989.

12   Judgement on *Mine Workers' Union versus BCL Mining Company*, 7 November 1989.

13   Industrial Court Judgement on *Debswana Diamond Company versus Mine Workers' Union*, 15 March 1995.

8 Class organisation and class struggles

Introduction

The previous chapter has examined the development of trade unions in terms of their qualitative and quantitative aspects. I have argued, following Marx, that the trade unions are the real organisations of the working people, in which the workers carry on their daily struggles with capital. By organising in the course of the struggle, the working class becomes a self conscious class, that is, a class for itself, and the interests it defends become class interests. The object of this chapter is to show how workers in Botswana have striven, within the limits imposed on them by the capitalist state, to assert their autonomy and to challenge the capitalist system.

As indicated in Chapter 7, the trade union movement in Botswana accepts the reality of the capitalist system. The challenges that the trade unions pose to the capitalist system are not to eliminate the system but to defend the immediate social and economic interests of the workers. That is, to counteract the tendency of capitalist production to push the value of labour to its bare minimum. To this end workers have resorted to illegal strike actions in a deliberate defiance of the law. It is argued that these challenges by the workers, although expressed in purely economistic terms, constitute class struggle. Most strikes and labour disputes are over wages or grievances related to wages. This is the result of a wages policy that stated that any increases in wages and salaries in all sectors of the economy must be kept in line with increases in wages in the public sector, and not so much with the rise in productivity. In a situation where the state, as the guarantor of private capital accumulation, intervenes in industrial relations and interferes with free collective bargaining, it transforms the trade union question into a class question, and a class question into a political question. The trade union struggles are no longer "pure and simple", but political struggles against the capital and the state.

The American economist Griffin (cited in Hyman, 1989, p. 17) defines a strike as a "temporary stoppage of work by a group of employees in order to express a grievance or enforce a demand". Expanding on this definition, Hyman (1975, pp.

115

19-25) points out three elements in a strike action: (a) a strike is a temporary stoppage and the workers intend to return to the same jobs with the same employer (who also normally views the stoppage in the same terms), (b) the action is a stoppage of work, and thus in principle at least distinct from an overtime ban or a go-slow, and (c) it is a collective action undertaken by a group of employees, and differs from refusal by tenants to pay rent or students to attend lectures, acts which are called strikes only by analogy. Hyman argues that an important characteristic which may distinguish different types of strikes is their duration. He makes a distinction between a "demonstration strike" and a "trial of strength" strike. According to Hyman, a demonstration strike is an industrial action which is short lived and lasts only a few hours or a few days. This type of action involves what he calls "perishable disputes". The primary purpose of a demonstration strike is to call attention to a grievance and strikers are usually willing to return to work to permit negotiations to take place even before concessions have been offered. Hyman argues that these types of strikes are prevalent in Britain, and have proven highly effective in speeding negotiations towards an acceptable outcome. On the other hand there is a strike action which functions as a "trial of strength" between employers and workers, and lasts several days or even several months. This type of strike action is rare.

The important thing to note about the strike actions in Botswana is that like strike actions in Ghana, Kenya and Zambia, they are normally about wages, conditions of service, unfair labour practices, and bad industrial relations at the work place. These are the usual concerns of trade unionism and they reinforce the arguments I have made that a strike is more of defensive action to protect the interests of the workers. Strikes are a challenge to the capitalist system, rather than a overt attempt to overthrow it.

Class conflicts in the private sector

(a) The bank workers' strikes

The first major industrial action by private sector workers after the enactment of the Trade Unions Act and the Trade Disputes Act of 1969 came on 25 November 1974, when about 700 members of the BBEU went on an illegal strike for about a week as a result of a deadlock in negotiations over wages and other conditions of service (Cobbe, 1977; Moyo, 1981). The dispute was about the pay differentials between local and expatriate staff salaries and the management's failure to implement the recommendations of a commission of inquiry on differentials between South African and Botswana rates that the trade union had argued were discriminatory. The banks, though British owned, were effectively managed from South Africa by largely white male South African managers. In 1970, the banks decided to increase only the salaries of the expatriates in the form of "special allowances". This was resented by the union, and the matter was taken up with the management in 1971. It was not until July, 1973, that a one man commission was asked to look into the dispute (Moyo, 1981). According to Moyo, the commission recommended that any differentials between the local staff and expatriates should be removed and that there should be one basic salary structure for all the employees, and that any allowances payable to expatriates must not be part of the basic salary. The commission also recommended that the local staff must be given back pay covering the period of the dispute.

By 1974, the banks had not fully implemented the recommendations. The union added more grievances to their original list and accused banks' management of retarding the pace of localisation. Another complaint was that the banks' wages and salary structures, which were pegged to those in government by the WPC, failed to take into consideration longer working hours worked by bank employees. The union argued its members could not be compared to state sector workers who work regular hours and argued that the comparison did not take into consideration fringe allowances paid to state sector workers. There was a deadlock and the union served the Commissioner of Labour with a strike notice. On 22 November 1974, two days before the strike, the minister banned the impending strike in an announcement in *The Government Gazette* (extraordinary). The strike was declared illegal in terms of the Trade Disputes Act, on the grounds that the union had not exhausted the requirements of the act. The workers resolved to go ahead with the strike anyway and the strike commenced as planned on the 25 November 1975 and went on until 2 December 1974. After a week, the management warned workers to return to work or face dismissals. Cobbe (1977) points out that in spite of the return to work by the strikers, the banks awarded increases in wages and salaries shortly thereafter. Cobbe speculates that the intransigence of the management could also have been influenced by the government's attitude that bank workers were already well paid compared to the majority of private sector workers and had no moral right to be asking for more pay.

The next major bank strike was in 1989, when some 592 workers belonging to Barclays Bank of Botswana went on a one week strike. The strike, which was described as the country's most devastating financial sector strike, was prompted by the bank management's decision to review the salaries and make a 10 per cent wage increment offer to managerial staff without following the procedures of the collective labour agreement.[1] According to the union, such review and increments were in violation of the collective labour agreement entered into by the commercial banks and the BBEU.[2] The Department of Labour failed to persuade the workers to go back to work, the Minister for Labour declared the strike illegal in terms of the Trade Disputes Act and the matter was sent for compulsory arbitration.

The Permanent Arbitrator found that indeed the bank's decision to make a salary increment without consulting the union was *ultra vires* the interests of the union. The arbitrator however upheld the management's decision to deduct two days wages from the strikers pay packet on the grounds that workers had continued with the strike after it was declared illegal.[3] It is not possible to estimate the financial cost of the strike to Barclays Bank, but it must have been substantial because thereafter the minister took the unprecedented action of declaring banking an essential service, effectively outlawing strikes in the financial sector.

In 1990, the National Development Bank Staff Union went on a four day strike against alleged corruption and mismanagement by National Development Bank's senior staff. The union also alleged that the bank's accounting system had collapsed. In the ensuing dispute, it was also discovered that top politicians in the ruling party, including President Masire, owed the bank vast amounts in interest payments. The Commissioner of Labour intervened and later referred the dispute to the minister. Whilst the matter was still pending, the state resolved to restructure the bank's operations, and in the process, about 130 workers lost their jobs. The employees had accused the management of corruption, mismanagement and nepotism. It was alleged that loan applications from top civil servants and ministers were not subjected to normal screening for project viability, and that some people in senior management of the bank were giving themselves loans which were also above what they would qualify for. In 1992 the bank was owed about P97,000,000 most of which was said to be irrecoverable.

(b) The mine workers' strikes

The first strike in the mining sector was at Orapa in 1974, when a group of machine operators and other workers went on a three day wildcat strike after a dispute over minimum wages. The Orapa Diamond Mine is a high yield, capital intensive extractive mining operation and is highly profitable to the De Beers group. According to Cobbe (1977) the workers had asked for a wage increase and the company was ready to accede to the request. However, the government intervened and said that the workers were already being well paid in terms of the wages policy. When the miners threatened to strike, the government backed down and allowed the management to increase wages.

The defining moment for Botswana 's labour relations came in July 1975 at Selebi Phikwe, where there was a large copper nickel mine involving huge financial resources from American Metal Climax (USA) and the Anglo American Corporation of South Africa. Since coming on stream in 1970, the mine had been plagued by a series of technical problems that greatly delayed production and thus affected government revenue (Cooper, 1978, pp. 244-277). The union had put forward a wage demand for a monthly minimum of R562 in their negotiations with the management. But the state, through the WPC, intervened and instructed that the appropriate minimum wages for Selebi Phikwe mine workers should be R40 a month (Ngidi, 1985). The management and the union could not come to any agreement concerning wage increase demands; there was a deadlock that was followed by a strike action. The strike was declared illegal in terms of the Trade Disputes Act. The striking miners locked the main gate to the main smelter plant and some sections of the miners attacked expatriates workers who were coming to work in company cars. Units of the paramilitary force were sent in to disperse the strikers and restore law and order in the mine. During the ensuing fracas, more than 600 people were arrested. After the strike the government authorised the management to fire all workers and re-employ them through a sifting process in which alleged ring leaders and "communists" were not re-employed (Cooper, 1978).

It was President Seretse Khama who seemed to give succour to the management to do whatever they wanted with the striking workers. The President claimed that he had knowledge that the majority of the workers did not wish to participate in the strikes but were intimidated by a "hard core of politically motivated individuals who hope to reap political rewards from the chaos which could result". President Khama expressed concern about workers who, he argued, though comprising only a minority of *Batswana*, were trying to hold the nation "to ransom" through wage demands. He said that such demands were not in the interests of the nation because these demands could scare away foreign investors. The President also said that it was essential for Botswana's development that the country should continue to retain foreign investment and that this could only be done if the companies which invest in the country were allowed to obtain "a reasonable return on their investment". The President pointed out that illegal and unnecessary strikes had continued to such an extent that Botswana would lose its reputation as a "stable and safe country to invest in".[4] Some 34 trade union activists were later tried and sentenced to terms of imprisonment raging from three to twelve months for charges including intimidation, riotous assembly and wanton destruction to property.

Class conflicts in the public sector

(a) *The manual workers' strikes (1968-69)*

Workers' struggles in the public sector have been spearheaded by the so called "industrial class employees", who are organised in the Manual Workers' Union - Botswana's biggest trade union. This union comprises the so called "unskilled" workers like drivers, cleaners, garbage collectors, grave diggers, cooks, security guards and messengers employed in central government, local authorities or parastatal organisations. Manual workers have a long history of militancy, and some people suspect that it was the manual workers' militancy which prompted government to amend the Constitution in 1969 and introduce tighter controls on organised labour (Motshidisi, 1975).

It was on 15 February 1968, that the Manual Workers' Union (then NUGMW), voted for a strike action which was to last for ten days. The government departments involved were the PWD Workshop in Gaborone, the Government Printer, the Central Stores, the Botswana Agricultural College and the Content Farm in Sebele on the outskirts of Gaborone. The trade union cited the source of their grievances as low wages, unfair dismissals and lack of proper protective clothing; it alleged that a clocking device had been tampered with to prolong the working day.[5] After the commencement of the strike, government issued a statement urging workers to go back to work as some of their demands had been met and that a commission of inquiry would be appointed to look into their other grievances like hours of work and protective clothing.[6] The workers ignored the appeal from the government and stayed away from work. Thereafter, the government issued an ultimatum that workers should return to work before the end of the following day or face dismissal. Only ten workers were reported to have returned to work before the deadline expired.[7] The following day a government spokesman announced that all workers who had not returned to work would have their contracts terminated and would lose their gratuity rights. The government also announced that those who wished to reapply for reinstatement could do so. Thereafter it was reported that all the strikers who had defied the government's ultimatum had "gone back to their respective departments to seek employment". The PWD was reported to have re-employed all workers whilst the Government Printer refused to re-employ seven of the twenty eight strikers.[8]

In the meantime negotiations between the union leaders and government continued behind the scenes with union leaders insisting that all workers must be employed without preconditions and that workers should not lose their gratuity rights. But government negotiators were adamant and insisted that workers who wanted re-employment must first reapply. The government also refused to back down on its position that all workers who went on strikes and had refused to heed government ultimatum had lost their gratuity rights.[9] However on 27 September the government backed down. The Minister of State, Mr M.P.K.Ngwako, told about 300 workers in Gaborone that government had decided that the workers who had been on strike would not lose their gratuity rights after all, although the days on strike would count against their leave.[10] Later it emerged that during the negotiations workers had threatened to call a nationwide general strike. But it is not clear whether this threat had carried any weight or what sort of compromise was reached behind the scenes. However, a few months after this strike, the secretary general of the same trade union was reported to had been warning trade union activists about the danger of indulging in politics and saying that the union had now decided in principle to persuade workers to cooperate with the government in the development of the country. The secretary general also warned the workers of the danger of ignoring their trade union.[11]

(b) The teachers' strikes

The position of white collar public sector workers is a vexed question. At the centre of the matter is that employment in the public sector, especially in the welfare areas like education, health and administration, is not directly or exclusively defined by capital-labour relation because these workers are more involved in the production of use values, rather than surplus values (Fairbrother, 1989). Fairbrother argues that state employment is a distinctive form of capitalist employment and that workers have increasingly displayed a capacity to organise and act in ways that indicate a recognition of their subordination as wage workers. He argues in the context of teachers struggles in Britain that:

> To appreciate the class position of the workers, it is necessary to consider the structural contradictions of their place in a capitalist society ... On one hand, workers in the welfare areas sell their labour power for wages as teachers, nurses, administrators, or clerical workers - on the other, these workers are employed in contexts where the "immediate purpose" of their labour is to produce use values, knowledge, health, shelter or to provide the means of participating in exchange relationships through income maintenance (p. 192).

In 1986 the Botswana Teachers' Union (BTU), the oldest workers' organisation, started to crumble as a result of internal disputes when its ability to represent and articulate the aspirations of its members was questioned by the more youthful and militant members.[12] For more than 50 years of its existence, the BTU had represented all members of the teaching profession in the country. However, in 1986 the secondary school teachers broke away to form their own teachers' organisation - BOFESETE.

At its founding congress, held under the banner of "Mobilise for a democratic teachers' federation", the secondary school teachers argued that the BTU was dominated by well paid headmasters of the older generation who were reluctant to challenge the state on any issue including conditions of service and pay. The teachers also argued that the organisation's leadership had abdicated its responsibilities to its membership because of its failure to challenge the government.[13] The secondary school teachers, who represented the young generation of *Batswana* teachers, had come to resent the old guard in the leadership. They argued that the entire executive committee of the BTU consisted of principals and head teachers who had benefited from the job evaluation exercise and were the happiest beneficiaries of the exercise. The teachers also accused the BTU leadership of being too complacent, timid, docile and acquiescent in its dealings with government, and that the BTU had been overtaken by events and had become irrelevant and could not adequately address issues that faced teachers in contemporary Botswana.[14]

BOFESETE's major grievance was low salaries. BOFESETE argued that the teachers were not being paid well and that they wanted to negotiate with government about their pay and other conditions of service. As pointed out above, for public sector workers (except industrial class employees), negotiation and collective bargaining are an anathema to the state, their employer. Thus when BOFESETE first presented an application for registration, the registrar refused to register the organisation on the grounds that its Constitution carried a clause which said that one of the objectives of BOFESETE was to negotiate with the government. After the offending clause was removed and other amendments made, BOFESETE was duly registered on 10 February 1987 as an association, in accordance with the Societies Act, and not as a trade union, as it would be the case under the Trade Unions and Employers' Organisations Act.

After registration, BOFESETE faced another challenge to its existence. It now had to battle for recognition by the Ministry of Education. Apparently, the old guard in the Ministry of Education, some of whom had been promoted to their jobs after long teaching experience, were not favourably disposed to the "rebellious and confrontational" organisation.[15] The chairperson informed the delegates that they had pleaded with the ministry officials and pointed out to them that by not recognising BOFESETE they were acting contrary to the spirit of Section 13(1) of the Constitution, but that their plea had fallen on deaf ears. The refusal to recognise BOFESETE seemed to have been spearheaded by the Permanent Secretary for Education, who was reported to have labelled BOFESETE a "divisive and sectarian organisation" and instructed all head teachers not to help BOFESETE with any facilities.[16] BOFESETE carried on, and toward the end of 1987 about 500 teachers, all claiming to be members of BOFESETE, refused to mark junior certificate examination papers, in protest against conditions of service. They argued that accommodation was poor, that the food was bad and served under unhygienic conditions, and that the pay for marking examination papers was too low.[17]

As the boycott continued, the ministry sent out letters to individual teachers threatening to charge them with insubordination and misconduct. The teachers, who were mostly university graduates, and therefore some of the most educated workers in Botswana, also saw an opening and tried to force a de facto recognition by the ministry. The strikers refused to have any dealing with the ministry officials except through BOFESETE. Its Secretary General, Serake Mfolwe, pointed out that the dispute could only be resolved by negotiations with BOFESETE. He argued that the striking markers were BOFESETE members and that the organisation was a legal organisation, whose Constitution clearly stated that it was the sole representative of the secondary school teachers.[18] BOFESETE was finally recognised by the new Minister of Education, R.Molomo and his new permanent secretary, P.O.Molosi, following a cabinet reshuffle after the 1989 general elections.

Despite this long journey to recognition, the formation of BOFESETE seemed to have opened the floodgates of militancy on the part of the teachers. On 24 November 1987, citizen lecturers at the Molepolole College of Education and at the Gaborone Polytechnic went on a two week strike and refused to mark examination scripts. Their grievances concerned salaries, housing and the slow rate of localisation. The strike was declared illegal in terms of the Public Service Act and the lecturers were ordered to go back to work, and disciplinary action was taken against the lecturers involved.

The biggest strike by white collar workers came in September 1989, when more than 10,000 primary school teachers went on a four week strike in order to press their demands for higher salaries. Unlike BOFESETE, which boycotted examination marking, the action by the primary school teachers amounted to a strike action in the classic sense. Like all other strike actions in the country, the strike was declared illegal by the Minister of Education.[19]

The background to the strike is that earlier that year, the mostly young primary school teachers followed in the footsteps of BOFESETE and broke away from BTU to form BOPRITA - a primary school teachers organisation. BOPRITA emerged spontaneously in protest against the recently completed job evaluation exercise. The teachers said that they were dissatisfied with the methods of the job evaluation which awarded more money to administrators like headmasters and principals, and less to teachers. During the debate on the job evaluation a majority of teachers, again mostly young teachers, became increasingly disillusioned with the leadership of the BTU for its failure to defend the interests of the teaching profession and resolved to go on strike.[20]

Amidst threats of dismissal by the Permanent Secretary for Education, BOPRITA instructed a firm of lawyers to proceed against the Minister of Education and the Director of the Unified Teaching Service and to ask the High Court to set aside as null and void the job evaluation recommendations as applied to primary school teachers. The grounds cited by the teachers were that the job evaluation exercise was *ultra vires* the laws under which they had been employed and in breach of their contract of employment with their employer, the state.[21] The case did not reach the court. Instead the ministry appointed a special task force to deal with the grievances. The main objective was to examine the grading of all members of the teaching service, with particular reference to primary school teachers, and to submit its report to the Ministry of Education for onward transmission to the cabinet.[22] The teachers were invited to send representatives and a compromise was reached.[23]

(c) The manual workers' strike (1991)

The most recent and biggest strike yet in Botswana's labour history was launched by this section of the working class in November 1991 when about 40,000 workers went on a one week strike following a breakdown in negotiations between the union and the state. This followed a dispute over wage claims and the interpretation of a collective agreement. Workers felt the government had reneged on an agreement reached to raise their wages from P237 to P600 per month, an increase of 154 per cent.

The wage negotiations had been going on for almost a year following the adoption of a new wages policy for regrading the public sector salary structure. As in the case in public sector employment these changes were not done through negotiations with the employees' organisations.[24]

According to Johnson Motshwarakgole, one of the union negotiators, when the government introduced a new wages policy, the union assumed that deregulation meant that wages would be determined through collective bargaining. On the basis of this assumption, the union appointed a subcommittee to devise a formula which the union could use in its negotiations with the government. According to Motshwarakgole:

> The subcommittee resolved that the best way was to negotiate for a living wages and decided to calculate the living wages based on official statistics on the cost of living. The subcommittee relied on what the CSO said was the basket of goods required to maintain an average family. To arrive at this the subcommittee went to the shops and costed the items in the CSO basket and arrived at the figure of P600. The union went to the negotiating table with this information, and demanded a living wages of P600 a month, or an increase of 154 per cent.[25]

After protracted negotiations lasting several months, the National Joint Industrial Coordinating Council (NJICC) - a statutory body made up of union leaders and senior government officials from the DPSM, agreed that the 154 per cent wage increase demanded by the manual workers was justified and reasonable. The NJICC then resolved to make recommendations to the "relevant authorities" for approval.[26]

However, according to the collective labour agreement between the Manual Workers' Union and the government, NJICC, which is chaired by the Deputy Director of DPSM, the second person in command of public sector employment, is the highest negotiating body.[27] It was the phrase "relevant authorities" that seemed to have caused a lot of confusion and much aggravation. For instance, the national organiser of the union, Motshwarakgole, when asked what he understood by the term "relevant authorities", was of the view that it meant that the agreement will be taken to the Minister for Public Service just for a "signature".[28] But what happened thereafter was a dramatic reversal of the "understanding" reached by the two parties.

After receiving the NJICC recommendation, the Director of the DPSM asked his colleague at the all powerful MFDP to give an opinion. In a secret memorandum that was later leaked to a weekly newspaper, the Permanent Secretary for Finance rejected the wage claim by the union, arguing amongst other things that the calculation of the living wages was erroneous and that the CSO basket shows that the poverty datum line (PDL) is in fact P328. He argued that the union had used average prices instead of minimum prices. The permanent secretary argued that the calculation of PDL assumes that people with lower income purchase goods from the cheapest possible source, but that the union has aimed at finding items which when added together would yield the P600 per month, thus justifying the 154 per cent wage increase demand. He further argued that in any case wage determination could not be based on the calculation of the PDL alone, but had to take into account factors such as labour productivity and affordability by the employer to pay a specific wage rate.[29] The permanent secretary further argued that there was no basis to argue that union members' productivity had increased, and that manual workers are already better off than their counterparts in the private sector, and that any wage increase would precipitate wage demands in the private sector, and would have a racket effect on the public sector salary structure.

When the workers learnt about this opposition from the treasury they felt that government had reneged on the collective agreement and voted to go on strike for one week. After two days, the strike was declared illegal in terms of the Trade Disputes Act, and the workers were warned to return to work or face summary dismissals. On the second day of the strike, it was announced that unless all striking workers went back to work the following day, disciplinary action would be taken against them in terms of the Industrial Class Regulations.[30]

The workers ignored the threats of dismissal and went ahead with the strike action. Four days after the warning, the government carried out its threat and sacked its industrial class employees en masse, and instructed the local authorities and parastatals to do the same in accordance with the Industrial Class Regulations. These state that any employee who absents himself from duty for two consecutive days without authorisation is automatically deemed to have terminated his services.[31]

For the whole of that week workers in Gaborone, which had the largest number of manual workers, would gather at the parking area of the African Mall, a small shopping area mostly for small businesses, where the headquarters of the BFTU was situated. The workers were joined by University of Botswana students who came to demonstrate their solidarity with the university branch of the Manual Workers' Union. The whole shopping area was like a carnival, with workers and students toyi-toying (a form of dance popularised by ANC cadres in South Africa) and singing, despite acts of provocation by units of the paramilitary Special Support Group, which deliberately drove through the chanting crowd several times.[32]

On the fifth and last day of the strike, there was an emergency cabinet meeting. After the meeting, it was announced through the radio station that all sacked employees were now advised to reapply for their old jobs but were told that they would lose all their benefits. This was interpreted as a softening of government previous hardline attitude.

The government's reaction to the strike was given by the Minister of Public Administration, in a written address to the Parliament. The minister said that beside the fact that the strike action was not procedural in terms of the union's own Constitution and the memorandum of agreement entered into between the union and the government, the strike action was also illegal in terms of the Trade Disputes Act.

The minister also pointed out that the wage demand was not in the national interest as it would have serious financial and economic implications. He said the wage increase would mean diverting resources that would otherwise have been spent on development projects such as building more schools, more roads and more clinics and reducing the general welfare of the nation as a whole.

Some of the reasons that the minister gave were: (a) that an increase of wages for manual workers would result in similar demands by similar categories of workers in the private sector where the salaries are even lower, (b) that such demands would result in marginal firms going out of business because of unaffordable labour costs, (c) that other firms may resort to automation, and (d) that such transmission of wage increase into the rest of the economy would result in Botswana becoming a high wages economy. This, the minister cautioned, would defeat the government's objective of attracting foreign investment.[33]

The union called off the strike after a week as planned in order to continue with negotiations. But instead of continuing with the negotiations, the MFDP announced that the government was going to appoint a Salaries Review Commission to look into public sector wages and salaries, and that the union would be invited to send representatives.[34] The union for its part decided to take the government to court and asked the High Court to declare the government in breach of the collective agreement, to order the government to abide by the agreement reached at NJICC, to declare the government lockout to be in breach of the collective agreement, and to declare the dismissal of all striking workers null and void, and unreasonable and unlawful.[35]

The judgement was a compromise. The court held that the matter was whether the decision of the NJICC had the effect of constituting a minimum wages of P600 per month or it was a recommendation. The judge said that he was unable to order the implementation of that decision, and ordered that it must still be taken to the "relevant authorities" for a final decision.

Significantly, the judge seemed to agree with the union that NJICC is the highest negotiating body. He even referred to both the speech by the minister responsible and the Director of DPSM's implicit recognition of the NJICC, but insisted that the earlier statement by the Deputy Director, together with a letter from the Director himself to the effect that though the decision had been reached the matter still had to be taken to the relevant authorities, left a reasonable belief that the matter was not finalised. The judge concurred that the NJICC's recommendation had aroused legitimate expectations on the part of the employees, but ruled that the strike was nevertheless unofficial in terms of the union's Constitution, and also illegal in terms of the law, and that the government's decision to lockout the workers therefore was not a breach of agreement. At the time of writing the Manual Workers' Union had decided to take the matter to the Court of Appeal.[36]

The most interesting aspect of this strike is that even before the matter reached the High Court, the government announced that it had made a policy decision to offer an option of permanent and pensionable terms of employment to all serving industrial class workers. The directive further stated that all new industrial class employees would from the date of implementation of the directive be appointed on permanent and pensionable terms and conditions of service, and would not have any other option as this would be their first contract with the employer. In other words the manual workers are now going be treated as white collar public officers and be governed by the Public Service Act and not the Trade Unions and Employers' Organisations Act.

This move by the state is significant because what lies behind it is the assumption that by dressing manual workers in white collar terms and conditions of service, the government will no longer have any trouble from them. The Public Service Act, as noted in Chapter 6, prohibits workers from forming and belonging to trade unions, or from bargaining collectively with their employer, the state. This also seems to be a strategy to demobilise and incapacitate the manual workers, and remove, once and for all, the irritation caused by this section of public sector workers.

Conclusion

A question may be posed as to whether trade union confrontations with the state and the capital really constitute class struggles. As I have shown these strikes have taken place mostly on the economic terrain. But the question needs to be posed and answered because it has important political ramifications. The strike actions described above have taken place in a legal environment that restricts free trade union activity, and in spite of the legal restrictions imposed by the state on strike activities. All these strikes have been declared unlawful and have ended up as "rebelliousness" against the state and no longer grievances arising from failure to reach a settlement in collective bargaining. The strikes have therefore been directed against both the capital and the state. This is because it is the legal procedures that often prevent workers from entering into any meaningful negotiations with the employer, and it is the state that is charged with the responsibility of enforcing the law.

Although some have argued that trade unions as institutions merely express class contradictions and do not challenge the existence of capitalism (Anderson, 1978), if the trade unions begin to break the law deliberately, then their actions become political.

As Marx (1968 a) argued, the existence of the organisation of the workers, that is, the trade union movement, is the *sine qua non* for political struggle. The fight for political power emanates from economic struggles. When the working class is not yet advanced in its organisation to undertake a decisive campaign against the ruling class, it must at any rate be trained for this eventuality by continued agitation against and hostile attitude towards the policies of the ruling class. Otherwise, Marx argued, the working class would remain heart-broken, weak minded, worn out and an unresisting plaything of the bourgeoisie, whose self emancipation may prove impossible. The fact that workers start by making the usual working class demands for higher wages and improved conditions of service, but choose to go on an "illegal strike" when these are not met, or when they find the legal procedures too cumbersome, suggests that the strike is as much against such laws and procedures as it is for the original demands. This action is never really planned with any great meticulousness and is certainly not very calculative.

In this regard I can reformulate the definition of a strike advanced by Griffin, and posit that a strike is a spontaneous stoppage of work as result of accumulated grievances from the work place, stored in the collective consciousness of the workers and aggravated by the negative response of the state and/or the capital. As this definition of a strike suggests, the grievances of the workers have to accumulate in their collective consciousness and be aggravated by the intransigence of the state and the capital. When the workers deliberately break the law of the land, thus expressing their disrespect for the state which is the upholder of such law, the conflict becomes political as well.

Waterman (1976, p. 331) points out that throughout industrial history, and across the contemporary world, the strike has been the most dramatic expression of wage protest, at once the most typical and the most extreme form in which the workers question their socially allotted role. Like volcanic rumbling and explosions, strikes provide information about fundamental social structures and processes that are concealed by the appearance of everyday industrial life. Strikes are the surface manifestation of an ocean of turbulent contradictions (Shaheed, 1979, p. 182). It is these "volcanic rumbling and explosions" that have continually shifted the balance of forces in favour of the working class, and as a result helped in the building of relatively better conditions of service and standard of living for the working class in some capitalist countries. It was through the workers' own struggles that workers' standard of living has significantly improved, not because of the benevolence of the state.

The final question that needs to be resolved in the light of the strike activities that I have described is, who has won in these confrontation between state and labour or between capital and labour?

The question posed in this way is false in the sense that it assumes that in the kind of struggles that I have analysed there has to be a total victory for one of the parties to the conflict. The reality is that both parties can claim victory, as they so often do. The labour movement can claim to have won the battle whilst the state and the capital can claim to have won the war. The reality of the situation is as described by Hyman (1989, pp. 22-3) when he argues that some strikes may end in capitulation by one side or the other, but usually a form of compromise is reached. Having endured the losses which a strike entails, both sides are normally determined to end with something to show for their pains even if unable to claim victory convincingly, and this would also have an impact on the state policy. How state policy can actually be affected by working struggles is the subject of the concluding chapter.

Notes

1   *Mmegi Wa Dikgang*, 21 April 1989.
2   *Mmegi Wa Dikgang*, 24 April 1989.
3   See the Permanent Arbitrator's judgement in Botswana Bank Employees' Union versus Barclays Bank of Botswana Ltd and others, 29 September 1989.

4   Seretse Khama's address to the nation on the Selebi Phikwe strike on 19 December 1975.

5   *The Botswana Daily News*, 19 July 1968.

6   *The Botswana Daily News*, 24 July 1968.

7   *The Botswana Daily News*, 28 July 1968.

8   *The Botswana Daily News*, 30 July 1968.

9   *The Botswana Daily News*, 30 July 1968.

10   *The Botswana Daily News*, 27 September 1968.

11   *The Botswana Daily News*, 28 June 1969.

12   *Mmegi Wa Dikgang*, 10 May 1986.

13   *Mmegi Wa Dikgang*, 7 July 1988.

14   BOFESETE Chairperson's Report at the Third National Congress, 11 September 1990.

15   Ibid.

16   *Mmegi Wa Dikgang*, 12 September 1987.

17   Ibid.

18   *Mmegi Wa Dikgang*, 21 November 1987.

19   *Mmegi Wa Dikgang*, 12 December 1987.

20   *The Botswana Guardian*, 22 September 1989.

21   A letter from Kgoadi and Partners (Attorneys) to the Attorney General, reference opk/fmg 02034, 12 September 1989.

22   *The Botswana Daily News*, 15 October 1989.

23   *The Botswana Guardian*, 6 March 1990.

24   *Ministry of Finance and Development Planning Personnel Directive*, No. 24/1990.

25   Interview with Johnson Motshwarakgole, National Organising Secretary of the Manual Workers' Union and member of the union negotiating team, 4 November 1991.

26   Minutes of the NJICC meeting of the 12 July 1991.

27   Industrial Class Regulations.

28   Interview with Motshwarakgole, op. cit.

29   A letter from the Permanent Secretary (MFDP) to the Director of Public Service Management. The letter was leaked to the weekly *Mmegi Wa Dikgang* (25 November 1991) and published in full by the newspaper. The editor and the reporter were charged under the National Security Act. The charge was later withdrawn.

30   Savingram reference DP 10/1/2/2 of 3 November 1991 from the Director of DPSM to all district commissioners and heads of departments, and savingram U.3/13 I(16) from the establishment secretary of the unified local government service to all town clerks, council and land board secretaries.

31   Regulation 8.19 of Chapter 8 of the Regulations for Industrial Employees, February 1988.

32   I made a point of going to the African Mall as a non-participant observer of the strike. On its first day, armed units of the Special Support Group drove their Land Rovers provocatively through the crowd but luckily, were ignored. Later Motshwarakgole complained about this behaviour.

33   Lt-Gen Merafhe's speech to the National Assembly, *The Hansard*, No. 105, November 1991, pp. 102-106.

34   Public Service Directive No. 14/1992, 16 December 1992.

35   Civil case No. 1604 of 1991, in the High Court of Botswana.

36   According to Motshwarakgole, a campaign was launched by the union to persuade members to refuse to accept the option offered by government, and the government has also despatched officers from the DPSM to go and explain to the workers the advantages of converting to the new status.

9 Prospects for organised labour in the 1990s and beyond

Introduction

Trade unions have been variously defined as continuous associations of wage earners for the purposes of improving the conditions of working life, or as independent employees' organisations whose main objective is to negotiate with employers in order to regulate the pay and conditions of their members (Farnham and Pimlott, 1990). The trade union movement has historically evolved from the development of wage labour which was ushered in by industrial capitalism. The capitalist mode of production, the separation of direct producers from the means of production, and the commoditisation of labour power are the antecedent material conditions for the emergence of the trade union movement. In other words, trade unions are a product of the capitalist system. In this regard the discussion on the political economy of Botswana and the economic growth policies of the postcolonial state, the consequent structural transformation and class formation, demonstrate this point. Like in other parts of the world where capitalist relations of production have emerged, trade unions in Botswana arose with the main objective to fight for the improvement of the conditions of work, to negotiate with the employers about pay and conditions of service of their members, and generally to protect the legal, social and economic rights of workers.

Socialists have not been content with just explaining the relationship between labour movement and capitalism, but have injected a more normative element in their theorisation and sought to explain what the role of the labour movement *ought* to be (Marshal et al., 1980). Karl Marx had at times argued that the workers' struggle against capitalism was just the beginning of the process of working class emancipation and the formation of a new society. To Marx, the first efforts of the workers to be emancipated was the trade union movement, which was also an essential expression of the antagonism that existed between the proletariat and the bourgeoisie; an antagonism that will lead to total revolution after which all classes and oppression disappear (Moses, 1990). But Marx's optimism about the

131

revolutionary potential of the trade unions was cautious. He cautioned that trade unions seemed to be too exclusively bent upon the local and immediate struggles with capital, and had not fully understood their power of acting against the system of wage slavery itself. He argued that the future of trade unions lay in them learning to act deliberately as organising centres of the working class in the *broad interests* of its complete emancipation. He put this point more emphatically in *Value Price and Profit* (Marx, 1968b) when he pointed out that workers must not exaggerate their everyday struggles with capital because in these struggles the workers are fighting with the effects, and not the causes of those effects. They are merely retarding the downward movement but not changing its direction, and are just applying palliatives and not curing the malady. Lenin (1902) was more sceptical about the revolutionary potential of labour organisations. While he acknowledged the necessity of the trade union movement, he also pointed out that the history of several countries showed that the working class tends to develop only trade union consciousness, that is, the conviction that it is necessary to fight employers and strive to compel the state to pass necessary legislation. Lenin argued that revolutionary consciousness cannot develop out of the spontaneous economic struggles of trade unions, but must be brought from outside the sphere of relations of production. These positions of Marx and Lenin lay the contours within which the organisation of the trade union movement varies. That is, the exclusive focus on local and immediate struggles with capital on one hand, and the struggles for the "complete emancipation" of the working class as a whole on the other.

Trade unions and the class struggle

While there is no consensus as to what constitutes a class struggle, it is generally accepted that these struggles relate to the distribution of the social wealth. Sandbrook and Cohen (1975, p. 199) argue that contemporary working class action in the African context, with its militant economism, should be understood in the context of the inequitable distribution of rewards in these countries. They argue:

> Consumptionism on the part of the workers is undoubtedly stimulated by the contradiction between the political class's command that unions restrain wages, and related demands in the public interests, and its practice of self enrichment and conspicuous consumption ... [Government,] backed by a growing bureaucratic and commercial class, will deny increases in wages and services while at the same time swelling the power, privileges and earnings of the dominant economic groups.

Hyman (1975) argues that conflict in industry conventionally centres around the distribution of its products and the level of wages and salaries. He argues that it is the social pressure that encourage workers to express their grievances and aspirations in economic terms rather than as demands for control and creativity in work. He argues:

> The pressures are reinforced by the institutional procedures of industrial relations: pay claims are readily negotiable, since they provide ample scope for bargaining and compromise, whereas non-wage demands often involve questions of principle on which compromise is far more difficult. Trade union officials, faced with the power of capital, are normally far happier pursuing demands which offer reasonable prospects of peaceful settlement; hence workers' organisations reinforce the bias towards wage consciousness.

Industrial conflict can take various forms, ranging from disputes over such issues as the supervisor's attitude to the work force, to disputes over pay determination. They involve such actions as late coming, boycotts, sabotage of equipment, absenteeism, go-slow, overtime ban and work- to- rule. Marx argued that economic conditions first transform the mass of the people into workers and their common situation and common interests then constitute them as a class in itself against capital. In the ensuing struggles, this class becomes united as the interests of individual proletarians are generalised into class interests, and their struggle become struggles of class against class. Trade unions are therefore the real organisations of workers in which they carry out their daily struggles with capitalism, and it is the organisation of workers on a class wide scale, that is in trade unions, that tends to politicise the struggle (Draper, 1978, pp. 87-8).

In his letter to Friedrich Bolte, Marx (1953, pp. 93-4) posited that the political movement of the working class has as its ultimate object the conquest of political power, but that this requires a previous organisation of the working class which arises from economic struggles and then develops into the political arena. According to Marx, every movement in which the working class comes out as a class against the ruling class and tries to exert pressure from without is a political movement. Here Marx used the example of the law of the eight hour day: if the economistic demands of the working class are put into labour legislation, they are political because the class would have succeeded in enforcing its interests in a form possessing socially coercive force, namely law. In Marx's view, economistic strikes and political struggles are on a continuum, rather than being the two sides of a coin.

Trade unionism in Botswana

The aims and objectives of the labour movement in Botswana can be inferred from the constitutions of the trade unions. The constitutions of most labour organisations emphasise welfarism. For example, the Manual Workers' Union, the most militant of Botswana's trade unions aims to obtain and maintain just and proper rates of pay or remuneration, security of employment and reasonable hours and conditions of work for its members. The Constitution of the BBEU states that the union will pursue joint consultation with the management at all levels in order to secure the greatest possible measure of effective participation by the union in all decisions affecting the working conditions of its members.

The public sector labour organisations are not different from their private sector counterparts. BOPRITA has as its objective to afford fair representation wherever and whenever matters pertaining to teachers are being discussed, to advocate professional training of teachers, and to secure humane conditions of its members such as decent accommodation and subsidised rent. The objectives of the BOFESETE are to promote, enhance and elevate the status of teachers in society, and to preserve the integrity of the teaching profession.

The Constitution of the BFTU, the mother body of the trade unions in Botswana, perhaps best sums up the aims and objectives of the labour movement in the country, and reflects trade unionist consciousness as opposed to revolutionary consciousness. The BFTU proclaims the goals of the trade union movement to be to fight for the rights of the worker to an adequate wages, to give a decent living wages to the worker and his family, for hours of work that will give the worker the opportunity of enjoying proper leisure, recreation and cultural development, for security of employment, free collective bargaining and protection and maintenance of agreements arising from collective bargaining. In pursuance of these goals, the BFTU seeks to maintain good relations between employers and employees through collective bargaining, to make representation on labour and trade union legislation and other matters affecting trade unions and workers in Botswana, to secure adequate representation on state apparatuses dealing with labour legislation and to participate actively in the development of Botswana in accordance with Botswana's national principles and objectives. What is more, the BFTU Constitution has been greatly imbued with the doctrine of liberal democracy that is contained in the Constitution of Botswana. The Constitution of the BFTU states that Botswana workers believe that freedom of thought, expression and association, guaranteed by the Constitution must form the basis of the relationship between the workers' organisations, employers and the state.[1]

To the extent that their constitutions emphasise welfarism and protection of the rights of their members, it can be argued that the labour movement in Botswana has accepted that it must work within the system of exploitative relations of production. However, this acceptance to work within the existing exploitative relations of production does not necessarily invalidate the argument that trade unions have a potential to transform society. The acceptance points to the limits of trade unionism at this present conjuncture. The willingness of trade unions to work within the existing relations of production is due to the fact that the working class is itself the product of such a system. The limits of trade unionism in Botswana are not unique to Botswana conditions, but are the limits of trade unionism in general. As Perry Anderson (1978) pointed out, trade unions are an essential part of the capitalist society because they incarnate the differences between capital and labour. They are dialectically both an opposition to capitalism and a component of it. They both resist the given unequal distribution of income and at the same time ratify the principle of an unequal distribution by their existence, which presupposes the existence of management. It is the capitalist system that has produced the working class and it is the capitalist system that is defining the parameters of working class action by all manner of control and concessions - in one word, by continually "habituating" the working class to support, or at least acquiesce to the capitalist system.

Trade unions and the state

In Chapter 1 it was argued that notwithstanding its capitalist character, the form of the state is determined not by capital alone but by a constellation of class and nonclass forces in a struggle. The working class is a particularly important aspect of this constellation for two major reasons: firstly, because of the strategic place of the working class in the labour process, and secondly, because of the political strength of organised labour in influencing the form of the state. Capitalism constitutes the mass of the workers as a class in itself; the development of trade unions begins to transform this class in itself into a class for itself. The economic growth policies of the postcolonial period and the consequent structural transformation that took place in the political economy introduced three related processes: industrialisation, urbanisation and proletariatisation. All these factors combined to give the working class and their organisations a much needed social weight (Fine, 1991). The social weight that the trade unions possess is demonstrated eloquently in their confrontations with the state and capital, given dramatic expression in strikes. Waterman (1977, p. 58) argues that Third World workers, through their trade unions, have shown immense capacity to act courageously against structures created by the state, thus proving that the trade unions are still the "typical and universal organisation of the workers, the one that they cannot do without, and through which they both discover and impose themselves on society". Insofar as capitalism fails to satisfy its economic and social aspirations, the working class is necessarily drawn into a class struggle. It is capitalism that compels and accustoms workers to struggle (Draper, 1978).

Zeitlin (1980) argues that the state is the product of the historically specific constellation of class and other social relations, and its policies are a distorted reflection of the struggles for the realisation of contradictory interests through the state. These are political struggles. One important element in the social weight of the trade union movement in liberal democratic capitalist countries has been the electoral power of the workers. Workers are not just workers, they are also voters. In a formally liberal democratic capitalist country like Botswana, with regular elections, trade unions may also have electoral significance if their members are mobilised around broad social issues concerning the interests of the majority of the people. Kelly (1988) has pointed out that several governments in Europe have been forced to accommodate the demands of the mass of the working class or face electoral defeat.

In Botswana the social weight of the workers was given expression in electoral setbacks to the ruling party. Political support for the opposition in the urban areas has been growing steadily since Independence. In the 1994 election the main opposition party, the left populist BNF won about 38 per cent. The vote for the BNF in urban centres alone was about 45 per cent.[2] The growing strength of the opposition in the urban areas is directly related to the disaffection of the urban voters, who are mostly workers, with the ruling party. Speaking at the official opening of the seminar on the revision of the labour law in 1990, the Minister of Labour stopped short of admitting this reason as a factor behind labour reforms. He argued that because of state intervention in industrial relations, there is a danger of labour disputes being politically exploited and of government being accused of taking sides, presumably with employers. The minister pointed out that the time had come for new and independent institutions to be established for the settlement of disputes and that government must ensure that a situation does not develop whereby economic inequalities lead to social and political unrest, thereby destabilising the country as a whole ... "This is a matter of balancing forces ...".[3]

Conclusion: social movement unionism

Though the labour movements of emergent capitalist countries in the nineteenth century Europe were the object of detailed analysis by Marx and Engels and were the subject around which they constructed their theory of social revolution, they never developed a systematic theory of trade unionism. They touched on the subject at various stages over a period of 50 years, with the result that any Marxist theory of trade unionism has to be culled out and collated from those many writings (Moses, 1990). However, Marx's article on the role of trade unionism, *Trade Unions: Their Past, Present and Future* (Draper, 1978, pp. 99-103) contains vital clues about his thinking and in my judgment points in the direction of what has now become known as social movement unionism. Marx argued that trade union struggles are a basic form of the working class struggle against capital; as such, trade union struggles are also political struggles. This view, however, does not represent the totality of Marx's perspective on trade unionism. Marx also cautioned trade unions against relying too much on economic struggles. He cautioned that economic struggles are only short lived. Trade unions, if confined to the economic terrain, will only be addressing the effects and not the causes of their economic problems. He pointed out that trade unions have kept too aloof from wider *social* and *political* movements. He injected a normative element in his analysis of trade unionism and argued that trade unions should not be confined to local and immediate struggles with capital, but should awake to their historical mission: instead of fighting for a fair day's wages, to act against the system of wage slavery itself. Marx argued that apart from their original purpose, trade unions should learn

136

to act as organising centres of the working class in the broad interests of its complete emancipation; to this end they should aid every social and political movement tending in that direction and consider themselves champions and representatives of the whole working class.

This was Marx's position and it is one which I am endorsing here. This position seems to have influenced Antonio Gramsci (1978, p.443) who argued that:

> The proletariat can become the leading and the dominant class to the extent that it succeeds in creating a system of alliances which allows it to mobilise the majority of the population against capitalism and the bourgeois state.

The implications of this statement as well as that of Marx are straightforward: the working class and its class organisation, the trade union movement must, in their struggles against capital, take on board the interests of other social forces, and generally combine their struggles with those other social forces striving to transform social relationships within civil society. This is particularly important because in liberal democratic capitalist regimes, civil society comprises a vast array of interest and pressure groups, held together by the overarching capital relation of domination and subordination. In other words, even if these other social forces are not defined by the capital relation, they nevertheless are dominated and subordinated by it. The working class therefore has natural allies in a society dominated by capitalism, although of course the support of these natural allies cannot be taken for granted but has to be nurtured.

The question, however, for the present is this: how is this task - the linking of the economic struggles of trade unions with wider social and political struggles - to be accomplished? According to Munck (1988, pp. 117-8), in countries such as Brazil, India and South Africa, trade unions have been increasingly reaching out to those sectors of the population which lie outside formal sector employment, such as rank and file church workers, women's movements, community movements and other organisations traditionally seen as outside the labour movement. He argues that there is a growing confluence of interests and a gradual overcoming of previous social and political barriers, as some of these movements turn towards labour and in other cases labour turns towards them. According to Munck, since the mid 1970s, neighbourhood movements in Brazil have sprung up in big cities like Sao Paulo and have provided workers with a social base for support in their struggles. The struggles have centred around issues such as housing, health care, running water and transport. He argues that the city was turned into a broad supportive network in which were constructed multiple and varied social spaces of solidarity.

In India permanent workers' unions have taken up the cause of temporary or contract workers and there have been cases of industrial and even white collar unions extending their organisations to include rural labourers. There have also been acts of solidarity of unregistered casual workers with the registered workforce. In the case of South Africa, Lambert (1988, pp. 32-5) argues that in the 1980s a brand of trade unionism evolved that entailed a redefinition of the traditional role of trade unions to include not only factory issues but also township living conditions. This necessitated alliances at both local and national levels, and linkages of campaigns on the shop floor to local and national campaigns to deracialise and democratise the South African state. According to Lambert, the main content of this brand of unionism was the conscious establishment of "structured" alliances with urban social movements at the local level and political movements at the national level to challenge the existing structure of capitalist dominance in the spheres of the economy, civil society and the state.

This brand of trade unionism therefore is in line with the strategies envisioned by both Marx and Gramsci, except for one thing. Whilst it is true that in South Africa for instance the trade union movement successfully linked its struggles with other social and political movements, this emerged under specific historical and political conditions of oppression, repression and state surveillance. It is only in India that this brand of trade unionism has emerged under conditions of formally liberal capitalist democracy, and with little success. This therefore demands an examination of concrete conditions that can influence trade union struggles and shape their form. For example, in liberal democratic capitalist regimes like India, there exist other forms of political expression. The shortcomings of Munck's account of the Indian situation is that it does not shed any light on how this brand of trade unionism articulated or related to political organisations such as the communist or social democratic parties, which are present in the Indian political landscape.

The difficulty of this brand of trade unionism in conditions such as those of India and Botswana is that the state has supported in a variety of ways - politically, legally and ideologically - the separation of politics from economic struggles. Trade unions are expected to confine themselves to economistic issues and the welfare of their members only; any political issues are supposed to be the responsibility of political parties.

Since the advent of liberal capitalist democracy in South Africa in 1994, there are growing signs that this brand of unionism is under threat, or at least in retreat. With the deracialisation and democratisation of the society, there is a decline in the main content of political unionism: factory issues are being separated from township issues, and linkages of campaigns on the shop floor to local and national campaigns for democracy are beginning to wilt. The ANC traditional allies, the South African Congress of Trade Unions and the South African Communist Party are being marginalised by the government as the pressure of international capital begins to mount on South Africa to privatise and restructure state assets. The South African experience demonstrates that overtly political unionism is a product of conditions of political repression and is not sustainable in a liberal capitalist democracy. The question that must be posed is not how economic struggles and wider social and political struggles can be linked, but rather, how economic struggles of trade unions and wider social and political struggles can be accomplished in a liberal capitalist democracy such as that of Botswana, India and the new South Africa?

The answer does not lie with overtly political unionism, as was the case with South Africa before 1994, but must be related to the material conditions. That is to say, while taking the statements of Marx and Gramsci as guiding principles on social movement trade unionism, its form will be shaped by concrete social conditions. But a consensus can be reached on the parameters of this brand of unionism: social movement trade unionism, as opposed to an overtly political movement trade unionism, is about how the traditional concerns of trade unions can be linked with broader struggles in contemporary liberal capitalism. It is a brand of trade unionism which struggles within and around wage work for better wages and conditions and for union control over the labour process as a whole, including the struggle for socially useful production. Such unionism should articulate with the movements of nonunionised or nonunionisable workers, take up social issues within the society at large, and work for the continuing transformation of all social relationships and structures (Waterman, 1993).

The prerequisite for such linkages is the recognition that workers' struggles are not the only struggles in society, and that these struggles are bound to founder unless they are linked to nonclass struggles. Previous chapters have indicated that Botswana is a country in urgent need of social reforms in many areas.

The first area is its industrial relations system. A large number of workers have been denied the right of forming and belonging to trade unions. These include the public sector workers, such as central government workers, teachers, nurses and other health workers, local government workers, and other workers such as agricultural and domestic workers who are presently denied trade union rights. The registered trade unions must realise that the exclusion of these workers from the ranks of the trade union movement is designed to cripple the registered trade unions themselves. It would therefore be a crucial strategic move if the BFTU demanded the right of these workers to form and belong to trade unions. Already teachers have taken the unprecedented step of engaging in strike action in the public sector, though the only support which they got from the BFTU was a message of solidarity. In future it would be helpful if such actions were backed by more concrete forms of support from the registered trade unions, including regular consultations, solidarity meetings, and financial and logistical backing. All these can be done within the existing legal framework. In addition the possibility of illegal sympathy strikes should also be considered.

The second line of manoeuvre is that of a war of position, à la Gramsci. This is to link trade unions struggles with community struggles and the struggles of non- or multiclass democratic movements in the country such as youth, ethnic minorities and women. The labour movement should also take up new social issues within the society at large, either as they affect the workers specifically or as they affect the community at large. Botswana is a developing capitalist society. Its rapid economic growth policies and structural transformation have created many social imbalances that go beyond the immediate concerns of the labour movement. For example, good physical and social infrastructure is biased towards capitalist urban enclaves as it is very poor in the rural areas where about 75 per cent of the people live. People still travel long distances to get to the nearest clinic, school or other social service centre. Agricultural subsidies still favour those with large cattle herds, and in the urban areas there is an acute housing crisis which has resulted in exorbitant rentals. In Gaborone alone some 50,734 people are on the waiting list for houses; there is no proper public transport and workers have to part with their meagre wages to get to work on expensive and badly run private taxis and minibuses.[4] Though Botswana has a high GDP and per capita income, the distribution of both wealth and income is highly skewed and there is a problem of child poverty and homelessness. The government is gradually introducing school fees, health care is no longer free and at the same time the government has increased military expenditure. The media, though formally free, is dominated by the ruling party.

These problems face the majority of the people in and outside formal sector employment; they provide a common ground on which the trade unions could take the initiative and reach out to the people at large. The most important factor is that, of all the organisations of civil society, trade unions possess an organisational and administrative infrastructure, collective identity, capacity to mobilise, and bargaining power through their potential to disrupt the economy. Trade unions, therefore, need to forge strategic alliances with at present weaker organisations of the civil society to increase their social weight. These strategic alliances will be the most effective demonstration by which the labour movement can convince others that far from being narrow and selfish, it aims at the emancipation of society as a whole.

The labour movement should also wake up to the fact that a liberal democratic capitalist society such as Botswana, with a competitive system of elections, offers prospects for a more favourable terrain of struggle than fascism, dictatorship or a one party state system. Fortunately, it appears that some trade unionists are already aware of the potential that Botswana's liberal democracy offers. For example, Ronald Baipidi, the Secretary General of BFTU, argues in connection with the recent amendments to the labour law that the ruling party is panicking because it has realised that it was losing seats, especially in the urban areas: "They acquired a political expert who advised them to bring the workers nearer, and to bring the workers nearer is to satisfy their needs".[5] Johnson Motshwarakgole, the National Organising Secretary of the Manual Workers' Union, had this to say:

> I think workers must participate in politics. We must listen to all parliamentary debates, and identify who says what, so that we can know who articulates our demands. By listening to parliamentary debates we will know who has our interests at heart. We will then inform our members in every constituency which Members of Parliament are for us and who are against us, and we will deal with them at the next election.[6]

Though workers may suffer defeats they still have the political space to push their demands and thereby shift the balance of forces in their favour. One of the ways that this can be done is for the trade union movement to come up with its own macroeconomic policy framework as the trade unions have done in South Africa and Zimbabwe, for example. Within Botswana this approach was adopted by the women's coalition prior to the 1994 general elections, when they issued the Botswana Women's Manifesto which articulated the demands of women and demanded certain reforms. The electoral losses of 1994 have forced the government to concede to some of the demands in the form of trying to get rid of archaic laws that oppress women. Trade union struggles can, therefore, be political as well as economistic. This is so regardless of the fact that their demands may not be explicitly posed in terms of the "class struggle".

Needless to say, there will be some very serious objections to the position I am advancing here from the "left" in the country on the grounds that what is being proposed here are social democratic reforms that are likely to blunt the revolutionary edge of the struggle, vitiate the workers' revolutionary impulse and prop up the capitalist system. I can only say that whilst a socialist revolution is certainly desirable, and may or may not occur in the future, the urgent task facing the labour movement is to wrest as many concessions as possible for the working people, now.

Notes

1   See the Preamble to the BFTU Constitution and Rules (f), (g), (h) and (n).
        The information of the aims and objectives of the trade unions discussed
        below has been gleaned from the preambles and from the sections on aims
        and objectives in their constitutions.
2   Report to the Minister of Presidential Affairs and Public Administration
        on the General Election, 1994.
3   Minister Balopi at the opening of the seminar on the Revision of the
        Employment Act and the Trade Disputes Act, August 1990.
4   A press release from the Botswana Housing Corporation in *Mmegi Wa
        Dikgang*, 8 April 1994, p. 20.
5   Interview with Baipidi, 27 August 1991.
6   Interview with Motshwarakgole, 4 November 1991.

Bibliography

Ahmad, A. (1983), "Imperialism and Progress", in Chilcote, R. and Johnson, D. (eds.), *Theories of Development: Modes of Production or Dependency*, Sage Publications: London.

Alavi, H. (1972), "The State in Postcolonial Societies: Pakistan and Bangladesh", *New Left Review*, No. 74, pp. 59-81.

Althusser, L. (1971), "Ideological State Apparatuses", in *Lenin and Philosophy and Other Essays*, New Left Books: London.

Altvater, E. (1978), "Some Problems of State Interventionism: The 'Particularisation' of the State in Bourgeois Society", in Holloway and Piccioto (eds.), *State and Capital*, Edward Arnold: London.

Amin, S. (1987), "Preface", in Nyong'o, P. A. (ed.), *Popular Struggles for Democracy in Africa*, Zed Books: London.

Anderson, P. (1978), "Limits and Possibilities of Trade Union Action", in Clarke, T. and Clements, L. (eds.), *Trade Unions Under Capitalism*, Harvester Press: London.

Badie, B. and Birnham, P. (1983), *The Sociology of the State*, University of Chicago Press: Chicago.

Bates, R. H. (1971), *Unions, Politics and Political Development: A Study of Mine Workers in Zambia*, Yale University Press: New Haven.

Bean, R. (1985), *Comparative Industrial Relations: An Introduction to Cross National Perspectives*, Croom Helm: London.

Beckman, B. (1981), "Whose State? State and Capitalist Development in Nigeria", *Review of African Political Economy*, Vol. 23, pp. 37-51.

Best, A. C. (1970), "General Trading in Botswana, 1890-1968", *Economic Geography*, No. 10, pp. 598-611.

Billig, M. (1982), *Ideology and Social Psychology*, Basil Blackwell: Oxford.

Bjorkman, B. et al. (1978), "Types of Industrialisation and the Capital-Labour Relation in the Third World", in Southall, R. (ed.), *Trade Unions and the Industrialisation of the Third World*, Zed Books: London.

143

Borhaung, K. (1992), *Politics, Administration and Agricultural Development: The Case of Botswana's Accelerated Rainfed Arable Programme*, Chr Michaelsen Institute: Bergen.

Braverman, H. (1974), *Labour and Monopoly Capital*, Monthly Review Press: New York.

Caire, G. (1977), *Freedom of Association and Economic Development*, International Labour Organisation: Geneva.

Chazan, N. et al. (1988), *Politics and Society in Contemporary Africa*, Macmillan Education: Basingstoke.

Chenge, M. (1987), "The State and Labour in Kenya", in Nyong'o, P. A. (ed.), *Popular Struggles for Democracy in Africa*, Zed Books: London.

Clark, G.L. and Dear, M. (1984), *State Apparatus, Structures and Language of Legitimacy*, Allen and Unwin: Boston.

Clarke, S. (1991), "The State Debate", in *The State Debate*, Macmillan: London.

Cobbe, J. (1977), "Wage Policy Problems in the Small Peripheral Countries of Southern Africa, 1967-1976", *Journal of Southern African Affairs*, Vol. II, No. 4, pp. 441-68.

Cohen, R. and Henderson, J. (1991), "Work, Culture and the Dialectics of Proletarian Habituation", in Cohen, R., *Contested Domains*, Zed Books: London.

Cohen, R. and Hughes, A. (1978), "An Emerging Nigerian Working Class: The Lagos Experience, 1871-1939", in Gutkind, P. et al. (eds.), *African Labour History*, Sage Publications: London.

Colclough, C. and McCarthy, S. (1980), *The Political Economy of Botswana: A Study of Growth and Distribution*, Oxford University Press: Oxford.

Colclough, C. and Olsen, P. (1985), "Review of the Incomes Policy in Botswana: 1972-1983", unpublished consultancy report.

Cooper, D. (1978), "The State, Mine Workers and Multinationals: The Selebi Phikwe Strike, Botswana, 1975", in Gutkind, P. et al. (eds.), *African Labour History*, Sage Publications: London.

Crisp, J. (1984), *The Story of an African Working Class: Ghanaian Miners' Struggles, 1870-1980*, Zed Books: London.

Crouch, C. (1977), *Class Conflict and the Industrial Relations*, Humanities Press: London.

Crowder, M. (1988), *The Flogging of Phineus Macintosh: A Tale of Colonial Folly and Injustice, Bechuanaland, 1933*, Yale University: New Haven.

Damachi, U. G. (1974), *The Role of Trade Unions in the Development Process, with a Case Study of Ghana*, Praeger Publishers: New York.

Damachi, U. G. et al. (eds.) (1979), *Industrial Relations in Africa*, Macmillan: London.

Davies, P. and Freeland, M. (1983), *Labour and the Law*, Stevens and Sons: London.

144

Draper, H. (1978), *Karl Marx's Theory of the Revolution*, Vol. II, Monthly Review Press: New York.

Duncan, G. (1989), "Introduction", in *Democracy and the Capitalist State*, Cambridge University Press: Cambridge.

Dunlop, J. T. (1958), *Industrial Relations Systems*, Southern Illinois University Press: Carbondale.

Dutfield, M. (1990), *A Marriage of Inconvenience*, University Paperbacks: London.

Engels, F. (1968a), "The Origin of the Family, Private Property and the State", in *Marx and Engels' Selected Works in One Volume*, Lawrence and Wishart: London.

Engels, F. (1968b), "Engels Letter to J. Bloch in Königsberg", in *Marx and Engels' Selected Works in One Volume*, Lawrence and Wishart: London.

Epstein, E. C. (1989), "The Question of Labour Autonomy", in *Labour Autonomy and the State in Latin America*, Unwin and Hyman: London.

Evans, P. (1982), "Reinventing the Bourgeoisie: State Entrepreneurship and Class Formation in Dependent Capitalism", in Skocpol, T. (ed.), *Marxist Enquiries: Studies of Labour, Class and States* (American Journal of Sociology, Vol. 88, 1978), pp. 210-47.

Fairbrother, P. (1989), "State Workers: Class Position and Collective Action", in Duncan, G. (ed.), *Democracy and the Capitalist State*, Cambridge University Press: Cambridge.

Farnham, D. and Pimlott, J. (1992), *Understanding Industrial Relations*, Cassell: London.

Fine, R. (1984), *Democracy and the Rule of Law*, Pluto Press: London.

Fine, R. (1991), *Beyond Apartheid: Labour and Liberation in South Africa,* Pluto Press: London.

Forrest, J. B. (1987), "The Contemporary African State: A Ruling Class?", *Review of African Political Economy*, Vol. 38, pp. 66-71.

Freund, B. (1988), *The African Worker*, Cambridge University Press, Cambridge.

Frimpong, K. and Olsen, P. (1985), "Labour Relations in Botswana", mimeo: Gaborone.

Gertzel, C. (1979), "Industrial Relations in Zambia to 1975", in Damachi, U. G. et al. (eds.), *Industrial Relations in Africa*, Macmillan: London.

Gladstone, A. (1978), "Preface", in Kassalow, E. and Damachi, U. (eds.), *The Role of Trade Unions in Developing Countries*, International Institute of Labour Studies: Geneva.

Gladstone, A. (1979), "Preface", in Damachi, U. G. et al. (eds.), *Industrial Relations in Africa*, Macmillan: London.

Gladstone, A. (1980), "Trade Unions, Growth and Development", *Labour and Society*, Vol. 5, No. 1, pp. 49-68.

Good, K. (1992), "Interpreting the Exceptionality of Botswana", *The Journal of Modern African Studies*, Vol. 30, No. 1, pp. 69-95.

Gossett, C. W. (1986), "The Civil Service in Botswana: Personnel Policies in Comparative Perspective", unpublished PhD thesis, Stanford University.

Gramsci, A. (1978), *Selection From Political Writings 1921-26,* Lawrence and Wishart: London.

Gregory, C. (1979), *Labour and the Law*, W. W. Norton and Company: New York.

Halpern, J. (1965a), "Empire Through the Desert - Bechuanaland", in *South Africa's Hostages: Basutoland, Bechuanaland and Swaziland*, Harmondsworth, Penguin Books.

Halpern, J. (1965b), "A Very Disreputable Transaction - Bechuanaland", in *South Africa's Hostages: Basutoland, Bechuanaland and Swaziland*, Harmondsworth, Penguin Books.

Harris, R. (1975), "Political Economy of Africa: Underdevelopment Or Revolution?", in *The Political Economy of Africa*, Schenkman Publishing: Cambridge.

Harvey, C. and Lewis, S. (1990), *Policy Choice and Development Performance in Botswana*, Macmillan: London.

Held, D. et al. (eds.) (1983), *States and Societies*, Basil Blackwell: Oxford.

Hyman, R. (1975), *Industrial Relations: A Marxist Introduction*, Macmillan: London.

Hyman, R. (1989), *Strikes*, Macmillan: Basingstoke.

Iwuji, E. (1979), *Industrial Relations in Kenya*, in Damachi, U. G. et al. (eds.), *Industrial Relations in Africa*, Macmillan: London.

Jeffries, K. (1991), "Public Enterprises and Privatisation in Botswana", a paper presented at a conference on "International Privatisation: Strategies and Practices", University of Botswana.

Jessop, B. (1982), *The Capitalist State: Marxist Theories and Methods*, Basil Blackwell: Oxford.

Jessop, B. (1990), *State Theory: Putting Capitalist States in Their Places*, Polity Press.

Jones-Dube, E. (1992), "The Influence of Entrepreneurs On Rural Town Development in Botswana", in Baker, J. and Pederson, P. O. (eds.), *The Rural-Urban Interface in Africa*, The Scandinavian Institute of African Studies: Uppsala.

Kassalow, E. and Damachi, U. (eds.) (1978), *The Role of Trade Unions in Developing Countries*, International Institute of Labour Studies: Geneva.

Kelly, J. (1988), *Trade Unions and Socialist Politics*, Verso: London.

Kennedy, P. (1988), *African Capitalism: The Struggle For Ascendancy,* Cambridge University Press: Cambridge.

Kirby, I. (1990), "The Role of the Law in Contracts of Employment and Settlement of Disputes", a paper presented at a labour seminar, 27 August 1990: Gaborone.

Kitching, G. (1987), "The Role of the National Bourgeoisie in the Current Phase of Capitalist Development: Some Reflections", in Lubeck, P. (ed.), *The African*

Bourgeoisie: Capitalist Development in Nigeria, Kenya and The Ivory Coast, Lynne Rienner Publishers: Boulder.

Klare, K. E. (1982), "Juridical Deradicalisation of the Wagner Act and the Origins of Modern Legal Consciousness", in Beirne, P. and Quiney, R. (eds.), *Marxism and the Law*, John Wiley: New York.

Kraus, J. (1979), "Strikes and Labour Power in Ghana", *Development and Change*, Vol. 10, pp. 233-57.

Kuznets, S. (1955), "Economic Growth and Income Inequality", *American Journal of Sociology*, No. 45, pp. 1-28.

Lambert, R. (1988), "Political Unionism in South Africa: The South African Congress of Trade Unions, 1955-65", unpublished PhD thesis, University of Witwatersrand.

Lebang, T. and Olsen, P. (1990), "Settlement of Labour Disputes in Botswana", mimeo: Gaborone.

Leys, C. (1976), "The 'Overdeveloped' Postcolonial State: A Re-evaluation", *Review of African Political Economy*, Vol. 5, pp. 39-48.

Lewis, S. R. and Sharpley, J. (1988), "Botswana's Industrialisation", IDS discussion paper, University of Sussex.

Liato, B. (1989), "Organised Labour and the State in Zambia", unpublished PhD thesis, University of Leeds.

Lubeck, P. (1987), "The African Bourgeoisie: Debates, Methods, and Units of Analysis", in *The African Bourgeoisie: Capitalist Development in Nigeria, Kenya and The Ivory Coast*, Lynne Rienner Publishers: Boulder.

Machayo-Omid, P. (1992), "Trade Union/State Relations in Developing Countries; Its Impact on Trade Union Capacity to Safeguard Workers' Interests in Kenya", unpublished MA thesis, University of Warwick.

Marshal et al. (eds) (1980), *Labour Economics: Wages Employment and Trade Unions*, Richard Irwin: Massachusetts.

Marx, K. (1968a), "The Eighteenth Brumaire of Louis Bonaparte", in *Marx and Engels' Selected Works in One Volume*, Lawrence and Wishart: London.

Marx, K. (1968b), "Value, Price and Profit", in *Marx and Engels' Selected Works in One Volume*, Lawrence and Wishart: London.

Marx, K. (1981), *A Contribution to the Critique of Political Economy*, Progress Publishers: Moscow.

Marx, K. and Engels, F. (1953), *Letters To Americans: A Selection, 1848-1895*, International Publisher: USA.

Marx, K. and Engels, F. (1968), "The Communist Manifesto", in *Marx and Engels' Selected Works in One Volume*, Lawrence and Wishart: London.

Marx, K. and Engels, F. (1970), *The German Ideology*, Lawrence and Wishart: London.

Miliband, R. (1989), "Marx and the State", in Duncan, G. (ed.), *Democracy and the Capitalist State*, Cambridge University Press: Cambridge.

Mogalakwe, M. (1983), "The State and Class Formation in Botswana", unpublished MA dissertation, University of Essex.

Mogalakwe, M. (1986), *Inside Ghanzi Freehold Farms: A Look at the Conditions of Basarwa Farm Workers*, Ministry of Local Government and Lands: Gaborone.

Mogalakwe, M. et. al. (1996), "Labour Relations in the Public Sector in Botswana", a paper presented at a regional conference on public sector labour relations in Southern Africa: Harare.

Molutsi, P. and Holm, J. (1990), "Developing Democracy When Civil Society Is Weak: The Case of Botswana", *African Affairs*, Vol. 89, No. 356, pp. 323-40.

Molutsi, P. et al. (1993), "The Report of the Study of the Trade Unions and the Botswana Federation of Trade Unions", mimeo, University of Botswana.

Moses, J. A. (1990), *Trade Unions Theory From Marx To Walesa*, Berg Publications: New York.

Motshidisi, K. (1975), "The History of Trade Unions in Botswana", Part 1 and Part 2, mimeo: Gaborone.

Moyo, N. (1981), "The Application of Incomes Policy in the Private Sector", in Harvey, C. (ed.), *Papers On the Political Economy of Botswana*, Heinemann: London.

Munck, R. (1988), *The New International Labour Studies: An Introduction*, Zed Books: London.

Nafziger, E. W. (1988), *Inequality in Africa: Political Elites, Proletariat, Peasants and the Poor*, Cambridge University Press: Cambridge.

Nafziger, E. W. (1990), *The Economics of Developing Countries*, Prentice Hall: New Jersey.

Ngidi, G. (1985), "The History of Botswana Mine Workers Union (BMWU)", unpublished BA dissertation, University of Botswana.

Parson, J. D. (1980), "Political Economy of Botswana", unpublished DPhil thesis, University of Sussex.

Parson, J. D. (1984), *Botswana. Liberal Democracy and the Labour Reserve in Southern Africa*, Westview Press: Boulder.

Parson, J. D. (1990), "The 1989 Botswana General Elections' Results and Selected Issues of Botswana's Political Economy", mimeo: Gaborone.

Parsons, Q. N. (1975), "The Economic History of Khama's Country, 1844-1930", in Palmer, R. and Parsons, Q. N. (eds.), *The Roots of Rural Poverty in Central and Southern Africa*, Heinemann: London.

Parsons, Q. N. (1993), "Botswana: An End to Exceptionality?", The Round Table 325.

Parsons, Q. N. et al. (1995), *Seretse Khama 1921-1980*, Macmillan: London.

Pickard, L. (1985), "From Bechuanaland to Botswana: An Overview", in *The Evolution of Modern Botswana*, Rex Collins.

Pickard, L. (1987), *The Politics of Development in Botswana: A Model For Success*, Lynne Rienner Publishers: London.

Pinkney, R. (1993), *Democracy in the Third World*, Open University Press: Buckingham.

Pritt, D. (1970), *Employers, Workers and Trade Unions*, Lawrence and Wishart: London.

Richards, A. and Waterbury, J. (1990), *A Political Economy of the Middle East: State, Class and Economic Development*, Westview Press: Boulder.

Salamon, M. (1987), *Industrial Relations. Theory and Practice*, Prentice Hall: New York.

Sandbrook, R. (1975), *Proletarians and Capitalism: The Kenyan Case 1962-70*, Cambridge University Press: Cambridge.

Sandbrook, R. (1982), *The Politics of Basic Needs*, Heinemann: London.

Sandbrook, R. and Cohen, R. (1975), *The Development of the African Working Class*, Longman: London.

Saul, J. (1974), "The State in Postcolonial Societies: Tanzania", in *The Socialist Register*.

Selabe, B. (1988), "Citizen Investment, Its Role, Opportunities and Constraints", a paper prepared for the National Conference on Strategies for Private Sector Development, August, 1988: Francistown.

Shaheed, Z. (1979), "Union Leaders, Workers' Organisation and Strikes: Karachi 1969-72", *Development and Change*, Vol. 10, No. 2, pp. 181-204.

Simkin, C. (1975), "Labour in Botswana", *South African Labour Bulletin*, Vol. 2, No. 5, pp. 28-35.

Spalding, H. (not dated), "United States Labour Policy Foreign Policy and the Role of the American Institute of Free Labour Development", a paper presented at the Brooklyn College, City University: New York.

Stedman, S. J. (1993), "Introduction", in *The Political Economy of Democratic Development*, Lynne Rienner Publishers: Boulder and London.

Strinati, D. (1979), "Capitalism, the State and Industrial Relations", in Crouch, C. (ed.), *State and Economy In Contemporary Capitalism*, Croom Helm: London.

Taylor, J. (1977), *From Modernisation to Modes of Production: A Critique of Sociologies of Development and Underdevelopment*, Routledge and Kegan Paul: London.

Thirlwall, A. P. (1989), *Growth and Development with Special Reference to Developing Countries*, Macmillan Education: Basingstoke.

Thompson, D. and Larson, R. (1978), *Where Were You Brother? An Account of Trade Union Imperialism*, War On Want: London.

Todaro, M. (1989), *Economic Development in the Third World*, Longman: London.

Todaro, M. (1992), *Economics for a Developing World*, Longman: London.

Warren, B. (1980), *Imperialism, Pioneer of Capitalism*, New Left Books: London.

Waterman, P. (1976), "Third World Strikes: An Invitation to a Discussion", *Development and Change*, Vol. 7, No. 3, pp. 331-44.

Waterman, P. (1977), "Workers in the Third World", *Monthly Review*, Vol. 29, No. 4, 1977, pp. 50-64.

Waterman, P. (1993), "Social Movement Unionism: A New Union Model For A New World Order?", *Review*, Vol. XVI, No. 3, pp. 245-78.

Zeitlin, M. (1980), "On Classes, Class Conflict, and the State: An Introductory Note", in *Classes, Conflict and the State: Empirical Studies in Class Analysis*, Winthorp Publishers: Cambridge, Massachusetts.

Ziemann, W. and Lanzendorfer, M. (1977), "The State in Peripheral Societies", in *The Socialist Register*.

Index

accumulated grievances 127
administrative bureaucratic state 13
aristocracy 34-36, 105

BCSA 92-93, 99, 101
BDC 45-46, 52
beef exports 50
BFTU 68, 71-73, 75-76, 85-88, 90,
    93, 95, 101, 103-105, 125, 134,
    139, 140
BOCCIM 86, 89, 105, 107
BOFESETE 93, 121-123, 134
BOPRITA 93, 123, 134
bourgeois democracy 40, 95
bourgeois nationalism 36

capital accumulation 2, 3, 7, 16-17,
    19, 23, 29, 33, 39, 47-48, 52-54,
    59, 66, 68-69, 80, 82, 86, 115
capital-labour relation 120
civil society 5-7, 9-10, 30, 137-138,
    140
class consciousness 98, 103
class interests 2, 38, 103, 113, 115,
    133
class organisation 98, 115, 137
class rule 7-9, 16

collective bargaining 4, 15, 18, 20-
    21, 57, 60, 76, 91-93, 105-107,
    115, 121, 123, 127, 134
collective consciousness 127-128
collective labour agreements 22, 89,
    99
Combinations Act 14-15
common interests 2, 39, 74, 133
community struggles 139
comprador class 10
compulsory amalgamation 20
compulsory arbitration 19, 21, 89-90,
    95, 117
compulsory registration 19
conspicuous consumption 50, 64, 132
Credit Sales to Natives Proclamation
    27, 36
Crown Lands 27, 47

demonstration strike 116
deregulation 123
diamond 45-46, 72, 75-77, 112, 118
disclosure of information 105-107
disputes settlement 4

economic crimes 50
economic growth 1-3, 16-17, 29, 33,
    40, 43, 45, 52, 54, 62, 65, 68, 76-
    77, 80, 82, 98, 131, 135, 139

essential services 20, 89, 91
European Advisory Council 35
exploitation 4, 8, 13, 45-46, 66, 113

FAP 48-49, 52-53
floor of rights 4, 69, 83
foreign reserves 28

Ghana 19, 37, 71-72, 95, 116
globalised accumulation 12
Grenelle Agreement 15

habituation 4, 69, 74, 77, 105
HIES 63-64
hut tax 27-28, 35

ideological habituation 4, 74
imperialism 7, 10, 12, 25
income distribution 4, 48, 54, 62-63, 65
industrial action 1, 70, 89-92, 104, 116
industrial class employees 101, 119, 121, 125-126
industrial peace 68-69, 74-76
industrial relations system 16, 18, 80, 82-83, 93, 95, 105, 139
infrastructural development 3, 11, 14, 29, 33, 46, 52, 54, 57
infrastructure 3, 26, 28-29, 39, 45-46, 139-140
international capital 12, 38-39, 46, 51, 53, 138
International Monetary Fund 12

Joint Advisory Council 35

Kenya 13, 19, 21, 71-72, 95, 116
Khama, Seretse 27, 37-38, 68, 72, 74-75, 119
kgosi 34-35
kgotla 34-35

labour control 1, 15, 17, 19, 21-22, 31, 69, 74, 84, 94, 105-106
labour discipline 19, 68
labour disputes 105, 110-111, 115, 136
labour productivity 56, 77, 124
labour repression 2, 5, 80-81, 88, 95
labour resistance 1, 21-22
liberal capitalism 3, 139
liberal democracy 5, 28, 30, 134, 140
living wages 124, 134
local accumulation 12

Manual Workers' Union 101, 107, 108, 119, 124-126, 133, 140
Matante, Philip 37, 82
Meaney, George 74
metropolitan capitalism 10-11
migrant labour 28
militant economism 132
minimum wages 56, 58, 83, 118, 126
Motsete, Kgalemang 36-37
Mpho, Motsamai 37

Namibia 25, 27
national bourgeoisie 2, 10, 12, 45, 47-50, 52
national development 2, 18, 39-40, 54-55, 64, 68-69, 74, 76-77, 109-110, 118
national interest 1, 2, 4, 14, 17-19, 45, 69, 74, 77, 125
National Labour Relations Act 15
nationalism 2, 30, 36
Native Administration Proclamation 27, 35
Native Tribunals Proclamation 35
necessary services 91
NEMIC 57, 60

parallel rule 35
parastatal organisations 59, 119
parastatals 45, 56, 58, 60, 92, 101, 125

peripheral capitalist development 2, 56, 62
perishable disputes 116
political unionism 5, 19, 138-139
private capital accumulation 3, 17, 23, 29, 33, 39, 52-53, 59, 66, 69, 80, 86, 115
profit maximisation 17
public enterprises 3, 99
public sector 4, 13, 44-45, 52, 56-60, 82-83, 92-95, 99, 101, 111, 115, 119-121, 123-127, 134, 139

revolutionary consciousness 132, 134
RIDS 48, 63

Salary Review Commissions 60
sectionalism 103, 105
social inequality 62
social movement unionism 5, 136
social weight 1, 135-136, 140
South Africa 25-29, 35-37, 40, 51, 60, 99, 111, 116, 118, 137-139, 141
state elite 19, 22-33, 68-69, 73, 74, 76-77
state intervention 2, 4, 16, 31, 45, 54, 136
state regulation 19, 33

state-labour relation 2-3, 6, 13-14, 16, 22-23
state-society relation 6, 23, 30
strikes 4, 15, 18-19, 21-22, 82, 89-91, 115-116, 118-120, 127-128, 133, 135, 139
structural changes 2, 28
structural transformation 2-3, 29, 33, 98, 131, 135, 139

tax evasion 50
Trade Union Congress 69

wage labour 4, 8, 13-14, 65, 77, 98, 131
wage restraint 4, 18
wages policy 3, 54-60, 62, 66, 76- 77, 95, 115, 118, 123
working class 1-4, 6-7, 12, 14-15, 17, 22-23, 28-29, 31, 47, 66, 68-69, 74, 77, 92, 95, 98, 103, 105, 112, 115, 123, 127-128, 131-137
World Bank 12, 45
world capitalist system 2
WPC 57-60, 117-118

Zambia 19-21, 71-72, 116
Zimbabwe 25, 141